EMOTIONAL INTELLIGENCE

Develop Empathy and Increase Your Emotional Agility for Leadership. Improve Your Social Skills to Be Successful at Work and Discover Why It Can Matter More Than IQ | EQ 2.0

BRANDON BRADBERRY

Table of Contents

Introduction...9

Chapter 1: Emotional Intelligence 14

What is Emotional Intelligence? 14

Elements of Emotional Intelligence.......................................17

Emotional Intelligence in Action...19

Chapter 2: What are Emotions For...22

What Is an Emotion 22

Basic Emotional Responses..24

Identifying Emotions 27

How Did the Reaction Affect You Later on?..........................29

Chapter 3: Emotional Brain 30

Chapter 4: Emotional Intelligence at Work...............................35

Importance of Emotional Intelligence in the Workplace.....37

How Do Hiring Managers Determine a Candidate's Emotional Intelligence?...41

Chapter 5: Improve and Enhance Empathy: Connect Naturally With Others..44

What is Empathy? 44

Common Traits of an Empathic Person 44

Improving Your Empathy 46

How Highly Sensitive People Manage Their Emotions.........48

Understanding the Potential of Being Empathic, Controlling Overwhelming Feelings 50

Chapter 6: Social Awareness Strategies 54

Mastering Social Awareness 55

Chapter 7: How Emotional Intelligence Affects Your Motivation.......... 59

Chapter 8: Practical Exercises to Develop Emotional Intelligence 65

Reflecting on Your Feelings 65

Make a Note of Your Triggers.. 66

Keep track of the emotional triggers!.. 67

Making use of those emotions 68

Take a Timeout When You Need It 69

Start Practicing Responding 69

No Room for Superiority.. 70

Avoid Overthinking... 71

Writing Down Your Feelings 71

Chapter 9: Practical Ways to Be Happy and Enjoy Life...................... 73

What Is Meditation? 75

What Is Mindfulness?... 77

Chapter 10: Applications of Emotional Intelligence.......................... 81

Chapter 11: Dealing with a Partner Who Has Low Emotional Intelligence... 89

Strategies to Improve and Rescue Relationships in Both Your Work and Personal Life 91

Chapter 12: Managing Your Emotions 96

Understanding Your Emotions.. 96

Getting a Handle on Your Emotions.................................. 98

Using the EQ-i 2.0 Tool.. 102

Chapter 13: Understanding Emotional Drain and Energy Vampires.... 104

Signs of Emotional Drain 105

Types of Energy Vampire 109

Chapter 14: Observing and Expressing Your Emotions 113

Chapter 15: Boost Your Social EQ with These Powerful Verbal and Non-Verbal Clues 117

Body Language 117

Tone 123

The Speed of a Speech 125

Chapter 16: How to Control Negative Emotions.................... 126

Eliminate Negative Thoughts.. 126

Overcome Stress and Anxiety 129

Overcome Social Anxiety and Shyness 131

Chapter 17: How Emotional Intelligence Can Make You More Productive 135

Chapter 18: Developing Emotional Intelligence.................... 140

Developing Self-Awareness 140

Journal Your Emotions 141

How to Improve Emotional Intelligence?.......................... 142

How to Master Self-Regulation.. 144

Chapter 19: Why do we have Emotions?... 149

Realizing the Roles of Emotions in Human Existence 149

Components of Emotions.. 150

What, then, are the Roles of Emotions in Human Beings?................ 151

Effects of Negative Emotional Spills on Our Existence as Human
Beings.. 156

Chapter 20: Learn to Deal with Your Feelings 158

Recognizing and Managing Emotions 158

Chapter 21: Practical Ways to Use Emotional Intelligence.................... 165

Communicating and Dealing With Your Feelings 168

Chapter 22: Why is Emotional Intelligence so Vital to Ensure Success?
.... 172

Chapter 23: Emotional Intelligence and Self-Esteem 180

Emotional Intelligence - A Conscious Solution 182

Negative Impact on Business.. 184

Developing Emotional Intelligence Skills 185

Chapter 24: Different Types of Emotions: Negative and Positive........ 186

Chapter 25: Busting the Myths About Emotional Intelligence 191

Chapter 26: Tips, Tricks, and Skills to Improve Your Emotional
Intelligence.. 199

Emotional Intelligence Skills 199

Emotional Intelligence Tips & Tricks... 201

Chapter 27: Self-Perception & Emotional Intelligence............................208

Chapter 28: Releasing Destructive Emotions and Strengthening   Positive Ones..212

Chapter 29: NLP and Thought Reframing...221

Chapter 30: Dealing with Your Past...230

Chapter 31: The Art of Effective Communication....................................236

Conclusion..245

Introduction

Many people feel disconnected, causing them to seek methods of forming closer bonds to those around them. Modern methods of interconnecting can keep people in contact with those that matter to them, but interactions may seem brief, artificial, and lacking that closeness that empathy can provide. The bonds that come from truly relating to someone, from walking a day in their shoes as a character famously said in To Kill a Mockingbird, these ties cannot be underestimated as they stem from tapping into a potential that represents part of our legacy as human beings. This potential is called emotional intelligence, and it is a capability set that is directly correlated with personal success.

Emotional intelligence can represent the dividing line between someone who experiences life through close connections and interactions with others and simply lives. This capability can lead to a drastically improved quality of life as it can help men and women to infuse empathy into their lives. By having empathy for others, you can have more beneficial interactions and more positive, leading to outcomes in your own life, happiness, and personal success.

Emotional intelligence refers to the ability to recognize the feelings of others, to make distinctions between different emotions, and the ability to use emotions as a guide for behavior. It should come as no surprise that this quality first began to be appreciated in the 60s when people started to perceive the world through different tinted lenses. It took almost thirty years for the idea to enter common parlance, and it has taken off in the last 15 years.

Humans are social creatures, which means that understanding emotional intelligence and using it correctly is not only a boon but necessary. Something as simple as your facial expression, the position of your arms, how you are standing, and your eyes—all of these can be emotional indicators to others. It can influence how others perceive you and the overall result of the interaction. Although no one can be expected to be conscious of every centimeter of their bodies at all times, by paying attention to the cues that we send others, we can not only have more beneficial interactions but also demonstrate empathy.

Many people may be reading this book because they are curious to learn how their lives can benefit from emotional intelligence, and much of that benefit comes from having empathy. One of the things that make human beings so unique is that we can act altruistically— that is, we can perform actions that have no direct benefit to ourselves. This may include donating of time or money to a cause that we care about, helping someone on the street, or giving a hand to someone at work even if it might be detrimental to ourselves. These are ways that we show others that we care, and they are based on empathy.

Much has been said about the distinction between emotional intelligence and empathy, and the distinction is not always clear to people, even those that use these terms commonly. In truth, empathy is a critical component of emotional intelligence. In the last 20 years, many psychologists and others have attempted to create measures of emotional intelligence, and much of these measures attempt to gauge is how empathic men and women are. Part of the difficulty in distinguishing between emotional intelligence and empathy stems from a general lack of empathy.

Empathy, in part, comes from successfully honing the twin abilities of correctly assessing another person's mental state based on their own subjective experience and showing compassion both within your headspace and in interactions. Empathy, therefore, is a part of what is traditionally thought of as emotional intelligence, although empathy extends beyond merely having sympathy for others. Empathy also requires that we have empathy rather than merely show it. That is that we experience the subjective emotions of others rather than merely relate to their experiences. Emotional intelligence is thought of as a distinct skill that individuals can acquire or hone. This is sometimes contrasted with empathy, which some people are thought to have while others simply do not. Some readers may be familiar with the idea of the empath: a person who experiences the emotions and subjective experiences of others deeply. These empaths are thought to represent the idea of empathy being something intrinsic and particularly strong in certain people. Yet there is no reason why emotional intelligence should be a trainable skill while empathy is not. Indeed, with experience and training, people often become better at showing empathy because they get into the habit of trying to feel what others feel.

It is important not only to distinguish empathy from emotional intelligence but to distinguish empathy from the closely related sympathy. Sympathy is the ability to show tolerance and compassion, while empathy also implies that the individual relates to and experiences the feelings that the other person feels. Empathy, therefore, involves feeling sympathy for others while also experiencing their feelings. Honing emotional intelligence requires that you are skilled in empathy. As we will see in a moment, most models of emotional intelligence used by psychologists perceive empathy as being one of several skills that fall under the personal intelligence umbrella.

Empathy is important because studies suggest that empathy can confer several benefits in our personal and professional lives, which will be explored in this book. Studies have shown, in particular, that empathy is a critical skill in an effective leader. Leaders often have difficulty with demonstrating to their teams that they relate to them and that they care about their concerns. This leads to debate within the group and a lack of motivation. By showing empathy successfully, a leader can instill confidence in their leadership within the team while also pushing themselves towards success.

Chapter 1: Emotional Intelligence

You are not a robot. You can feel. This is why people, events, and situations evoke different emotions in you. Sometimes the gap between your emotions and reactions seems so negligible that you react to these emotions before realizing. At other times, you are more conscious or deliberate about your reactions. But as an intelligent human, your behavioral responses shouldn't be at the beck and call of something outside your control. Indeed, you can choose your responses by widening the gap between emotion and reaction. To achieve this, you need to improve an aspect of human intelligence known as emotional intelligence.

What is Emotional Intelligence?

Emotional intelligence is your ability to recognize and manage emotions within you and others. It is being in constant touch with your inner state of being or frame of mind and the things that trigger these emotional states.

Every emotion you feel is a form of feedback. A highly emotionally intelligent person can take the information provided in the feedback to influence their behavior in positive ways. The feedback can also be used to relate better with those around them.

Conversely, people with low levels of emotional intelligence rarely pay attention to the feedback from their emotions, especially at the initial stages. When they do, it is usually late. At that point, they simply let go of the oars and allow the strong currents of what they feel sweep over them and cause havoc or hopefully lead to good.

Your emotions can temporarily freeze your ability to think rationally and make you behave in ways that you will regret later. For example, someone did something that made you so mad that you acted rashly before realizing you shouldn't have said or done what you did. When regret becomes a constant feature in your daily life, it indicates a low level of emotional intelligence. You are not living to your full capacity as an intelligent human being. Something else is in the steering wheel of your life, and you need to change that fast!

You can be rich, famous, powerful, and brilliant, but without emotional intelligence, there is a yawning gap in your attitude that needs to be filled. Your intelligent quotient (IQ) can get you all the accolades in the world, but to be truly great and successful, you need a high level of emotional intelligence. In other words, you are an emotionally intelligent person if:

- You are fully aware and in touch with your emotions for most of your day. You are rarely taken aback by stressful people or situations.

- You can be intentional about your responses as a result of being aware of your emotions.

- You respond to and influence others intelligently.

- On the other hand, your emotional intelligence level is low if:

- You can't stand people. You are easily offended and react hastily.

- When you look back, you always blame yourself for not responding as you should. You were either too harsh or too soft. You seem to be carried away by how you feel at any moment, and your feelings instead of rational thinking heavily cloud your decisions. You feel bad and judge too quickly, or you feel good and make rash decisions.

- You are not willing to consider other people's viewpoints. You tend to be always rigid about your ways. You have a made-up mind even before you seek other people's opinions.

- People think of you as an excellent professional but a poor friend. You find it difficult to connect with people beyond the surface level. You think of other people as the tools you need to achieve your aims or as a means to an end.

- You do not inspire and influence people positively. Instead, you live your life mostly in reaction to others. You might have a great fortune, but you live an unhappy life.

Elements of Emotional Intelligence

Briefly, emotional intelligence comprises of five fundamental components, namely:

1. **Self-Awareness**: this refers to the ability to recognize and understand your emotions and feelings accurately, and how they affect your disposition or frame of mind. Essentially, it is the first tool you need to identify your strengths and weaknesses to know the part of your life that need work. Getting better at every other aspect of emotional intelligence depends largely on how well you can use the self-awareness tool.

2. **Self-Regulation (Self-Management):** this is the ability to hold yourself back from reacting to the first random impulse that occurs to you. It takes a lot of practice to gauge different situations rationally before responding consciously. Self-regulation or self-management is not about muzzling your emotions. Instead, it is about threading the middle path between primitive reactions and temperateness.

3. **Self-Motivation:** this is the ability to propel yourself forward regardless of challenging situations. Self-motivated people don't easily throw in the towel, get disoriented because of uncomfortable emotions, or give less than their best under pressure.

4. **Empathy (Social Awareness):** this refers to the crucial skill of identifying and understanding how other people feel. Managing how you feel while being oblivious of how others feel can damage your relationships. Being socially aware requires putting empathy into practice in all your interactions and relationships. With the right amount of empathy, you can place yourself in other people's shoes to feel and understand their perspectives. But because it is a delicate skill to master, it can easily be misunderstood and abused.

5. **Social Skills (Relationship Management):** this is the ability to build stronger relationships by recognizing and managing the emotions of other people and influencing them positively. It is an offshoot of developing sound social awareness and a natural consequence of bringing all the other components together. It is a vital skill for improving communication, effectively handling and resolving conflicts, and dealing with awkward situations.

To become a well-rounded human being, you need to work on all of these components consciously. Since they are closely linked, improving one aspect usually results in an overall improvement in all the other aspects.

Emotional Intelligence in Action

High emotional intelligence is not merely an abstract subject; it shows up in real-life behaviors. The following are only but a few out of the many ways it manifests. These are some of the difficult aspects of emotional intelligence. Recognize them and find ways to practice them more often in your life to get better at using them.

1.   **Forgiveness**: You can give other people the chance to hold your emotions hostage when you refuse to let go of past hurts. Resentment is anger turned inward – the only person getting hurt is you! Unfortunately, those with a low level of emotional intelligence can't seem to recognize that fact. Those who cause your emotional pain may have long moved on, but if you don't forgive, you won't heal from that emotional wound. When you forgive, you demonstrate a high level of emotional intelligence and set yourself free to move forward.

2.   **Bringing the Best out of Others**: When you commend, encourage, compliment, appreciate, and inspire people, you are meeting one of the most innate emotional needs of humans – the need to be acknowledged. Emotional intelligence enables you to focus on people's strengths instead of their weaknesses. Since we all crave acknowledgment, it is natural that people will feel drawn to you if you recognize and appreciate them. But besides wanting to be around you, the constant focus on their strengths makes them get better while minimizing their shortcomings.

3.   **Giving Helpful Feedback**: Emotional intelligence helps you present criticism in a way that allows the recipient to see that you are focused on making them better clearly. Conversely, if you lack emotional intelligence, your criticism of others would be because they do not live up to your standards.

4.   **Taking Pauses**: Perhaps one of the most elusive practices of emotional intelligence is taking conscious pauses just before reacting. Taking deliberate pauses before responses is not a show of uncertainty, fear, or reluctance. Instead, it shows that you are mentally weighing your options before speaking or acting. It is an easy concept to understand theoretically, but difficult to put in practice. However, when you get the hang of this skill, you will save

yourself from making long-lasting decisions based on fleeting emotions.

Chapter 2: What are Emotions For

<u>What Is an Emotion</u>

In many years, psychologists and philosophers have been having a spirited debate on emotions and various types like happiness and sadness. They have been trying to determine their nature if perceptions about various philosophical dynamics or cognitive judgments are about the satisfaction of set objectives. Various theories in neuroscience explain several suggestions on how a human being's brain can generate emotions by combining bodily perceptions and cognitive appraisals. If something thrilling in your life happens to you today, it is natural and very normal to develop an array of emotions such as happiness or sadness if it is a painful situation. There is a dualist view traditional that explains that a human being's body consists of a soul and a body. In this case, the soul is believed to be the one that experiences all mental states and emotions. However, this view can be disregarded and just termed as a motivated inference or a wishful thought since there is no substantial evidence that immortality and the soul exist.

Today, there exist two main approaches, scientific approaches, that can be employed in coming up with an explanation of what emotions are and their nature. Cognitive appraisal theory is one of the approaches, and it explains that emotions can be said to be judgments on how the situation you are in currently meets the goals you have set. According to this theory, emotions such as happiness are believed to be an expression of goals being fulfilled.

On the other hand, sadness and emotions depict unfulfilled goals and disappointments in life and can refer to a form of anger towards a stumbling block to your goals. Another theory that tries to explain what emotions are is that of William James, together with others. They came up with an argument that emotions are just perceptions of various changes in your body in different situations. These body changes that depict emotions include mental reactions and physiological stages in life.

These two theories, psychological perception and cognitive appraisal can be integrated to develop a unified definition of emotions. With an understanding of these theories, it is crystal clear that the mind controls and determines all sensations and perceptions based on the different situations we are in. We can, therefore, describe emotions as one's mental state that is associated with their nervous system linked to the chemical changes that take place in the body. These chemical changes are usually linked to your feelings, thoughts, degree of displeasure or pleasure, and behavioral responses. Emotions can also be termed as negative or positive experiences linked to certain patterns of physiological functions in the body. The bottom line is that emotions are responsible for all the cognitive, behavioral, and physiological changes that we undergo in our bodies and how we react to them.

Basic Emotional Responses

There are various types of emotions that have different natures and also varying influence in the way that we conduct ourselves when with other people and even generally how we live. These emotions, if not controlled, may tend to control us. They can even harm the choices that we make in life. Apart from that, these emotions are a determiner to what our thoughts are in different situations that we face daily. Understanding these emotional responses will also give us a strong foundation to advance, discussing how we can use them to rewire our bodies and minds to attain a better and healthier life.

Happiness

This is one of the emotions that people have used different approaches to attain; it thus tends to be vital. Happiness is referred to as a nice emotional state which depicts feelings of joy, contentment, well-being, gratification, and satisfaction. This emotional state is usually expressed through facial expressions like smiling, body language like a relaxed stance, and even a pleasing voice tone.

Sadness

This is another emotional state that is the opposite of happiness and is depicted by feelings such as grief, hopelessness, dampened mood, disinterest, and disappointment. This is a very common emotional state due to different stressful life experiences that we undergo daily. Having prolonged sadness might be hazardous to your health, specifically mental health, since it can advance over time to become fatal depression. Its severity usually varies as it depends on the cause and the extent at which you can cope up with it.

Fear

Fear is a very powerful emotional state that plays a vital role in one's survival. When faced by danger or any situation that seems threatening, you will get into a flight or fight response situation. At this point, you will find that your muscles become tensed and with an increased heartbeat and respiration rate. This will trigger you to either fight the danger or run away from it instead. This emotion is usually depicted by widening eyes and other psychological reactions like rapid breathing and heartbeat.

Disgust

Disgust is an emotional state that happens when you are disappointed or bored due to failure to achieve something. It can also be as a result of unpleasant sight, smell, or taste. This emotion can be depicted by the tendency to move away from disgusting you, other reactions like retching or vomiting, and even facial expressions like curling your upper lip. This emotion might even make you forever hate something that once disgusted you, which can be hazardous.

Anger

Anger is one of the greatest and most powerful emotions depicted by agitation, hostility, antagonism, and frustration. Just as fear, it is also capable of triggering your flight or fight response. There are various ways in which anger is usually displayed, and they include facial expressions like frowning. Body language, like turning down someone in a harsh manner, can also be a sign of anger.

<u>Identifying Emotions</u>

To use your emotions the right way, you need first to identify the emotions the right way. Let us look at the best way to identify the emotions:

Understand the Trigger

The first step towards identifying the emotion is first to know what caused it. This will help you to describe the events that led to an emotional event. In this step, try to stick to facts alone.

You can write down the event that led to the emotion to have it clear in your mind.

Why Do You Think It Happened?

The following step is to identify the possible causes that led to an emotional event. This is crucial because it determines the meaning that you give to the situation that happened. The type of emotional event that led to the issue will determine how you react to the event in question.

How the Situation Made You Feel?

The following step is to determine how the emotional event made you feel both physically and emotionally. This will help you see whether the emotion resulted in a positive or negative reaction.

You need to notice both the positive as well as the negative emotional and physical reactions that you felt when it happened. Notice any physical feelings that you experience, such as tightness in the body.

What Was Your Reaction?

You need to ask this question so that you understand your urges. However, for the process to be effective, you need to make sure you are completely honest. It might be painful to admit some of the urges that you felt when the event happened. When we face some situations, we, at times, get strange urges to react differently. Some of the emotions that we go through might make us regret it in the future.

You need to compare your reaction at the moment that things happened and how you usually react normally. This will tell you whether you managed to control the urge, or you failed to do so.

What Did You Do and Say?

The following step would be to understand what you said or did due to the emotions. Even though you didn't manage to respond correctly, you need to be honest with yourself about how you handled the situation. You also need to understand how the decision you made impacted on the situation. This can be a good learning experience for you.

Once you evaluate your reaction, you can then use the situation to learn how to handle another situation that might arise.

How Did the Reaction Affect You Later on?

The final step in identifying the emotions is to understand the consequences of the actions that you took. If you said some words during the event, how did they affect you? On the other hand, if you acted in a certain way, how did it affect you in the future?

So, if you find yourself being overly attached to your emotions after, you need to ask yourself what happened and take the time to observe how you react when it happens. Go through these steps so that you can recognize your emotions. Once you practice and get used to these steps, you will be able to identify your emotions the right way and then choose the best way to respond to situations.

Chapter 3: Emotional Brain

The brain is a grandmaster in manipulating emotions, so even when you think you know the basics of your feelings or emotions, it could be tricky. We like to think we are in control of our feelings and the triggers behind these feelings, but the truth is our brain has a much more profound impact than people like to admit.

Every single moment, there are lots of activities going on in your head, and the brain is in the middle of all these activities and somewhat complex processes. A lot of processes are involved in how we interpret situations and react to them. Remember that emotions are defined by three important things: cognition, responses, and reaction. The brain determines every one of these activities, which makes us wonder how our brain impacts our emotions.

What happens in your brain before you experience an emotion?
The first thing to know about your emotions is that it starts right from the brain. Emotions are a combination of our feelings, how we process these feelings, and our responses or reactions to those feelings. The primary purpose of emotion, according to Charles Darwin, is to encourage seamless human evolution. To survive, we

have to pass on our genetic information from generation to generation, which is why emotions are important.

Recognizing the importance of emotional experiences, the brain takes it upon itself to evaluate stimuli and activate a suitable emotional response. The brain reflects and considers the best way to respond to a situation so that the primary purpose of survival is achieved. It activates a suitable emotion as a response to propel the rest of the body to react accordingly. When you find yourself reacting to a situation with a kind of response, your brain is triggering the emotion it considers right for your survival right at that moment in time.

The brain is a vast network of complex processes that include information processing. One of the brain's primary network contains neurons which send signals from one part of the brain to the other. These cells or neurons transmit signals through what we call neurotransmitters; some kind of chemicals we either receive or release in the brain. The neurotransmitters are what make it possible for one part of the brain to communicate with another part. Dopamine, norepinephrine, and serotonin are some of the most examined neurotransmitters. Dopamine is the neurotransmitter that has to do with feelings of pleasure and rewards; it is the chemical that makes you happy when you do something good. This neurotransmitter is released as a reward for you to give a pleasurable and happy feeling.

On the other hand, serotonin is the neurotransmitter linked with learning and memory. It is believed to play a critical part in brain cell regeneration, and research has shown that an imbalance in serotonin can cause an increase in stress, anger, anxiety, and depression. Norepinephrine, on its own, helps modify your moods by controlling the levels of stress and anxiety.

Now, when there are an abnormal or unbalanced release and processing of either of these chemicals, there is usually a profound impact on your emotions and emotional state. For instance, when you do something that requires dopamine to be released and sent to the part of the brain responsible for information processing, but your brain doesn't process or receive the dopamine as it should, it could result in you feeling sad or mildly unhappy. Therefore, the abnormal release and processing of dopamine, serotonin, and norepinephrine have an immense impact on the emotions you have and the reactions you give to certain situations. The next time something which should have made you happy gives feelings of sadness, remember these neurotransmitters.

Again, your brain exerts influence on emotions because it is central to how emotions are formed. The brain consists of different parts that are all responsible for generating different emotions. The brain responsible for processing emotions is the 'emotional brain' which is generally referred to as the limbic system. The hypothalamus helps you regulate your responses or reactions to emotional triggers. Some parts of the brain, like the hippocampus, which all impact your emotions due to its memory retrieval functions. The hippocampus determines your emotional responses to triggers. Since different parts of the brain process, different types of emotions using different methods, damage to any part of the brain can have a huge influence on your emotions and moods, no matter how mild. Central to all of this is the limbic system, which takes a generalized and simple approach to stimuli.

The brain's left and right hemispheres also play important roles in emotion and responses. The hemispheres are responsible for keeping you functioning, but they also play a part in how you process information. The left hemisphere deals more with concrete thinking while the right hemisphere concentrates on abstract thinking. Because they both process information differently, the left and right hemispheres work together to manage emotions.

While the right hemisphere identifies an emotion, the left hemisphere interprets the emotion. For instance, when the right part of the brain identifies an emotion like anger, it alerts the left brain, making a logical decision in interpreting the context of the emotion and deciding the appropriate response to give. This is all a synchronized system, but if something goes wrong and one hemisphere can't do its job properly, it affects how you react to basic emotions. For example, if the right brain doesn't identify a negative emotion as it should, it prompts the left brain to become overwhelmed with the emotion without knowing how to respond.

Memory, whether long-term or short-term, is the function of the brain, and our memories dictate and inform our emotions. You get angry when you recall a resentful memory and get happy when you remember a pleasant memory. This is a continual process in the brain; it identifies a past emotion and then places you in a mood based on the emotion. So, when you get angry without knowing why, it may be your brain recalling some painful memory to initiate a negative emotion. How you can override this is to push yourself to think of things that have made you happy in the past. For example, if you are sad, simply thinking of some happy memories can trigger the release of dopamine, which rewards you with feelings of happiness.

Chapter 4: Emotional Intelligence at Work

Ever since the world started paying more attention to emotional intelligence, thanks to Goleman, there has been a segment of society that has been particularly engrossed in understanding what EQ can do for them. That segment is the business world or the corporate workplace. C-suite executives and hiring managers all over the world are keen to reap the benefits of emotional intelligence. Since the 1990s, there has been plenty of research to support the claims that emotional intelligence makes a person a better employee.

The baby boomers of the world did not care much for emotional intelligence in the workplace. They simply did their jobs, collected their paychecks, and went home. Today's workplace has changed. Millennials want more from their jobs than a mere paycheck.

Robert Walters, a recruitment company based in the United Kingdom, surveyed millennials seeking to understand various aspects of their jobs and professions. From this survey, the recruitment company determined that millennials are motivated by things that are different from what motivated them. Millennials are not content to settle for a job for the sake of having a job. Rather, they want a job that gives them a bigger purpose. They want to feel that they are fulfilled and growing. They want to feel like they are among a big community.

The millennial workforce also wants the freedom to plan their workdays without feeling as though they are under a microscope. They want to be able to be social in the workplace. They want a life outside of work, otherwise referred to as work/life balance. They also want to be rewarded for the things they do through pay increases, promotions, and recognition.

When compared to the older generations, it is clear that millennials have set quite a high bar. It is no wonder that hiring managers have sleepless nights trying to determine who is the best fit for their company. Against this dynamic backdrop, hiring decisions can no longer be influenced by IQ only. While hiring managers still want to hire smart candidates, they are being swayed more and more by emotional intelligence. In fact, in one survey carried out by Harris Interact for Career Builder, 75 percent of hiring managers said that they would rather hire an employee that is emotionally intelligent than one who has a high IQ. This is not to mean that hiring managers all over the world are united in downplaying book smarts. Rather, it shows that companies have finally come around because it takes more than knowing about the knowledge contained in books to survive in the workplace of today.

Importance of Emotional Intelligence in the Workplace

Emotional intelligence in the workplace is not just a fad that people are excited about that will go away after a while. There are true benefits to hiring an emotionally intelligent workforce.

Emotionally intelligent employees handle pressure better.

Just as the workforce of today is different from the workforce of yesteryear, the workplace has also changed. Before, workplaces tended to be more relaxed. The modern workplace looks to be more cutthroat and pressure-filled. With this in mind, hiring managers know that emotionally intelligent employees will be better placed to thrive in an environment of pressure. Imagine an environment where employees are unable to manage their emotions. What is likely to happen when a critical deadline is coming up? Probably lots of yelling and scapegoating. This would be a recipe for disaster.

Emotionally intelligent employees are better decision-makers.

Decision-making is an everyday activity in the business world. You need to make verdicts about how to solve client problems, which clients to pitch to, which colleagues to include in particular teams, how to format a report for a client, how to manage your workload efficiently, and many other decisions. The more emotionally intelligent you are, the more capable you are of making good decisions. When you know how to bring about your emotions, you can make decisions that are not simply emotional. Emotions are good and all, but they don't usually make for very good catalysts in decision-making.

For instance, you are a team leader working to deliver a project for a client. There is one colleague that is very good at performing financial due diligence, a skill that you need for this project. Unfortunately, this colleague does not like you, for reasons best known to them. They have made this clear to the extent of being publicly disrespectful. What do you do?

A person lacking in emotional intelligence might be tempted to engage in a power struggle with this colleague. After all, the colleague should respect the team leader regardless of their differences.

However, if you are emotionally intelligent, you will devise a way to deal with the colleague because you realize that getting into it with them is only going to ruin the progress of the team. You will figure out a way to play the role of a team leader without giving them an arsenal that they can use against you. Instead of playing their game, you will kill them with kindness. You will be fully invested in being the bigger person, and you will not allow a said colleague to drag you to their level. This is because you are self-aware, self-regulating, motivated from the inside, and well equipped with the social skills needed to handle a colleague that is behaving like a petulant child.

Employees with high EQ handle conflicts better

The workplace is a convergence of many personalities. When different personalities meet in one place, there is a high likelihood of crashing. Colleagues will not always get along. You may have potlucks or staff parties every other weekend, and they're still will be differences and conflict between the employees. In the face of conflict, you need employees that can resolve their differences with as little drama as possible.

High EQ employees are more motivated

Let's say you are a corporate owner who has worked hard to build your brand and hire a reasonable number of people to work for you. You invested your life savings into starting a company because you believed in your vision and mission. Two years after hiring your employees, you start to notice that all of them are coming in late, dragging their feet in their delivery to your clients, and sometimes not even showing up for work. Your brand starts to decline. Your clients are no longer satisfied. You feel defeated. Where did you go wrong?

You hired employees who were not emotionally intelligent.

Intrinsic motivation is a measure and component of emotional intelligence. Companies that hire emotionally intelligent people do not have to remind them to be motivated constantly. These employees are already motivated on their own and do not need the extra push.

Emotionally intelligent employees respond better to criticism.

Imagine having an employee that sulks every time they are criticized for something. How annoying would that be? As an employer, you do not have the energy or time to deal with employees who view feedback as a personal attack. Emotionally intelligent employees understand that there will be moments when they need to be corrected. Their self-identity and sense of worth are not pegged on what their boss has to say about them. They are secure in themselves and accepting of feedback, both negative and positive.

Outside of regular employees, workplaces also benefit from hiring emotionally intelligent managers. Such managers are better able to manage teams, communicate the vision of the company, and even resolve conflict. A manager that is low in EQ might cause the downfall of the company that they work for. Such a manager will try to impose their authority on the rest of the employees using intimidation, threats, and unwarranted tactics. The same goes for C-suite executives and anybody else that is in a management position at the workplace.

How Do Hiring Managers Determine a Candidate's Emotional Intelligence?

If hiring managers seek to hire candidates with high emotional intelligence, the question that naturally follows is this: How are they able to tell who is high in EQ and who isn't? Do they give a test? Are they silently judging you without your knowledge? It's more of the latter, but instead of judgment, it's more of an observation. You can tell a lot about a person without asking them direct questions.

Hiring managers will know if you are emotionally intelligent by checking how you have worked with teams in your previous roles. They will want to know how well you got along with these teams and whether you held any leadership positions in your past. Do not downplay the very important role this little fact plays in determining how the hiring manager sees you.

If you have been to an interview in the recent past, you were probably asked about a problem you faced and how you tackled it. Human resource divisions do not ask this question for the sake of entertainment or to fill space. Rather, they want to understand what approach you take when faced with challenges. Do you run and take cover, or do you face challenges head-on with equal parts courage and creativity? The reply to this question could very possibly mean the difference between being hired or receiving that infamous regret letter.

The other popular question that hiring managers love to ask is: *What is your biggest weakness?* This leaves many candidates to feel the need to lie that aiming for perfection is their biggest weakness. This reply has been given so often in interview rooms that recruitment teams have grown to anticipate it and possibly roll their eyes whenever they hear it. Now, whether you are the perfectionist you claim to be or not, the whole point HR is asking is because they want to know if you are self-aware. You need not lie about your weak points; you only need to demonstrate that you know what those points are. Of course, you also do not want to shoot yourself in the foot to demonstrate how self-aware you are. Saying that you often oversleep and arrive late for work is exactly how you do not get hired for the job.

Chapter 5: Improve and Enhance Empathy: Connect Naturally With Others

Giving a boost to your empathic abilities is an ideal way of increasing your emotional intelligence in the long run. At the beginning of this manual, we learned that empathy is a key element in emotional intelligence. For that reason, you cannot have a high EQ if you are not empathic.

What is Empathy?

Empathy refers to an individual's ability to listen and comprehend what they are feeling. This is a virtue that is essential for building strong relationships both at home and at work. People who lack this trait are often perceived as cold and distant. On the other hand, if you are an empathetic person, people will see you as loving and caring.

Common Traits of an Empathic Person

As you interact with people from all walks of life, certain traits will tell you that you are working with a compassionate individual.

Common personality attributes that will be evident in an empathic individual are briefly discussed.

Highly Sensitive

Guys with empathy will be highly sensitive. These are the type of individuals who will be there for you no matter what happens. They have a very solid background of what emotions you are working through. They can put themselves in your shoes. Unfortunately, the world is not so friendly and therefore, such people often get easily hurt.

Highly Intuitive

Empathic people will want to face the world with the help of their intuition. Before taking any actions, they will want to follow their guts. The exciting thing about this is that they approach life confidently. At times, this helps them enter into blissful relationships simply because they believed in their intuitions.

They Give too Much

They are being compassionate means that you can understand the emotions of other people. Therefore, a common trait of empathic individuals is that they love to give. Their act of giving is what drives them to help others out of their misery.

Need for Solitude

At times empathic people will be misunderstood due to their desire to be left alone. Their constant need for solitude is meant to help them connect with their inner selves. Eventually, this is what makes them self-aware of their emotions before understanding the feelings of others.

Improving Your Empathy

Considering the desirable traits of tenderhearted individuals, there are various ways in which you can learn to improve your empathy.

Get Feedback

Sometimes you need to ask other people about your social relations. Don't just assume that because people are smiling at you, they are happy. Get honest feedback from your friends and romantic partners. They will help you identify areas where you need to improve.

Listen

Active listening can also play a big part in enhancing your empathy. Through listening, you get to understand people better and reason out with them.

Smile at People

Never overlook the power of smiling at people. A keen eye should tell you that smiling is contagious. Science tells us that smiling liberates chemicals in the brain, which helps you maintain a good mood. As such, the act of smiling will not only help you increase health, but it will also boost your empathy.

Scrutinize Your Biases

Equally, you should consider scrutinizing your biases. These are the factors that often prevent you from being compassionate with others. For instance, you might fail to connect people because you prejudice them based on their gender, age, or race. To increase your empathic levels, try to examine your biases, and find a way of ignoring them. Ultimately, you will appreciate the importance of seeing people for who they are.

Challenge Yourself

It is also essential that you get out of your comfort zone to understand people better. Don't allow conversations to end abruptly; challenge yourself by bringing in creative and interesting topics that will spur real talks. Ideally, you will connect with people far beyond knowing about where they live.

How Highly Sensitive People Manage Their Emotions

Most people will attest to the fact that it is not easy to deal with emotions. It is an overwhelming task. Empathic individuals are known to be highly emotional. However, it begs to wonder how they effectively manage their emotions.

If you are a highly emotional person, it is imperative to learn how to deal with your emotions. This will confirm that your feelings do not blind you. Truly, at times you need to wake up to reality. Before you can empathize with other people, you need to understand your boundaries.

Put Yourself First

Without a doubt, putting your needs first might sound controversial because it is an uncommon trait of compassionate people. Nonetheless, for you to successfully take care of the needs of others, you need to begin by sorting your demands first. The clue here is that you should not be depleted. You should have the right energy to be able to see and help others out of their predicament.

Set Clear Boundaries

Sure, you are an empathic person. This does not mean that you can help everyone around you. You need to know that you are also human, with flaws. As such, set clear boundaries to help you know when to stop. People should also understand that you have limits.

Let it Go

Indeed, compassionate people will want to walk in the shoes of other people and give them a supporting hand to lean on in times of need. Similarly, when things are good, they will want to share moments of joy with them. In sad moments, empathic folks must learn how to let go. For instance, you might drain your energy when trying to mourn with a friend. In such instances, you need to embrace the idea of separation. There are some emotions that you need to separate yourself from. It might appear selfish, but in real sense you will also be helping yourself by managing your empathic nature.

Listen to Your Emotions

Another important step that empathetic people should remember to take is to listen to their emotions. You might be too focused on what others are feeling, and you could end up forgetting about yourself. For you to understand other people, you should first begin by comprehending and managing your own emotions.

Practice Celebrating

An individual who often listens and understands other people, you know what it means to feel happy. Also, you are fully aware of what someone can feel when they are in pain. Unfortunately, negative feelings will stick around for long as compared to happy feelings.

You should practice celebrating by reminding yourself of the good things you have achieved in your life. It doesn't have to be something big; honor any milestone you achieve as this will invite positive feelings your way.

Undeniably, having an empathic attribute will help you create blissful relationships with people since you can easily connect with them. However, you should not forget that you need to keep your life balanced. You need to pay attention to your feelings before committing yourself to others. First, manage your own before helping others.

Understanding the Potential of Being Empathic, Controlling Overwhelming Feelings

Besides people gaining the perception that you are too sensitive, there are numerous reasons why it is important to be empathic. Human beings can be unpredictable at times. When we watch the news and read the newspaper headlines, we often wonder how people can be so inhumane with their heinous acts. Building an empathic culture will, in the long run, help you grow your emotional intelligence. The mere fact that you can understand other people's feelings implies that you are emotionally smart.

Positive Vibe

There is a sensation that comes with knowing that you have helped other people deal with challenging situations. Being empathic will, therefore, invite positive feelings to your life. You might not be rewarded physically, but a compassionate nature always pays off.

Develop an Identity

People will always have an identity to relate to you with. If you are a cold person, they will simply know you for who you are. When in need of help, you can rest assured that most people will not want to help you. As a compassionate individual, you will develop a unique identity that tells a lot about how good you are. Again, this gives you a reason to be happy that you are making this world a better place to live.

Emotional and Physical Health

As people seek for ways of keeping themselves healthy and fit, they forget that empathy is a remedy. Well, this might sound strange since empathy is all about understanding people's feelings. Being empathetic means that you can learn more about how other people behave. Therefore, it gives you an opportunity of learning from others. By paying attention to people's feelings, you can adjust accordingly and live a healthier and happier life.

Additionally, connecting with other people is an important part of being a human being. Simply put, you have to create friends and learn how to live with them. Consequently, knowing how to effectively interact with others will keep you emotionally healthy as you can freely connect with those around you.

Lowering Stress

The virtue of being empathetic will also benefit you by helping you deal with stress. Bearing in mind that you can manage your emotions and those of others, it means you can handle stress better than other folks. You have been through tough situations since you have tried to understand others. Therefore, there is a high likelihood that you can challenge yourself and effectively handle stressful moments.

Conflict Resolution

Conflicts will always arise. This could occur in your private life or at work. Sometimes it is difficult to deal with conflicts because our differences blind us from realizing why it is vital to compromise. An empathic person will listen and comprehend why others are angered. They will treasure the importance of finding solutions above anything else. Consequently, through their compassionate nature, they will prevent conflicts from escalating.

Supporting Socially Desirable Values

There is no single negative social value that could be linked to empathy. The idea of being empathic promotes socially desirable values. These are individuals who want the best for people around them. They desire to see people collaborate, understand each other, and, most importantly, heal themselves.

Accordingly, there is great potential in being empathic. Some might perceive you as emotionally weak, but in the real sense, you are stronger. You are more in tune with your emotions, and therefore, you can be recognized as an emotionally intelligent person.

The sheer fact that you can connect with others more profoundly means that you create the perfect example of being a human being—part of being compassionate means that you treasure connections over disconnection. Living and connecting with people is what defines us as human beings. Without the associations we have made to this point, we wouldn't have been where we are.

Chapter 6: Social Awareness Strategies

It is essential to pay attention to ourselves and our feelings. But once we have mastered those, we can start to become more socially aware with a skill to pick up on the feelings of others.

Being socially aware will require you to be conscious of the world we live in, how it directly impacts some people, and how we all have different pasts and emotions. Social awareness requires you to recognize that one person might believe a certain thing because of how they were raised. You also have to understand how hard it might be for them to change that way of thinking because of the implications or belief settings. Even though you might believe something true, that doesn't mean that others will see things in the same light.

Social awareness requires you to understand what other people are needing while having the ability to come up with strategies that help them. You should see when people are hurting, struggling, or in pain on an emotional level while understanding what tools they might need to help them feel better. You can't cure their mood right away, but you can help them find something they need to make them feel better.

Mastering Social Awareness

The first step of becoming socially aware is realizing that you do need to be more conscious of the needs of others in the first place. Everyone is responsible for themselves, of course, but you also need to be conscious of how you're affecting others and what you might do that directly impacts other people. You have to figure out the needs of others that you care about, especially to ensure that you are taking care of both you and them.

Then, you can start to pick up on what people are thinking and find ways to manage the situation better. Look for ways to improve your social awareness in all interactions, not just ones that feel more important to you. Remember, it's a practice, and the more effort you put in now, the more it will show positively later on.

Listen to Your Surroundings

Take in the world you exist in, the neighborhood that affects your world, and even how the room might play an influence on your emotions and how others are feeling. When someone seems snappy or distressed, ask yourself if it could be the place that you are at that is making them upset. They might not realize that the lighting in the room is making them anxious, but you can, so you could turn off a light and turn on a more soothing one to help alleviate their anxieties.

Recognize the diversity among certain individuals and allow yourself to be open to these different kinds of people. Some people might seem stubborn or stuck in their ways, and it feels like you can't reason with them. If you try to focus on their individual needs and determine what can be done to help them on a specific level, no one is too stubborn to change their views. You just can't influence them the same way you would a person that's more open to new ideas and beliefs.

Remember that different situations will have opposite effects on some people. Someone with a high EQ won't treat two individuals the same way because they understand just how different two seemingly similar people can be.

Be Open to Others

When we start to shut people out of our lives, we can start to create serious issues. There are some individuals that you might never want to be around and that you strive to avoid, and this can be fine. However, if you don't let new people in your life and shut others out right when you meet them, it will affect you in the long run.

Don't separate someone from your life just because they seem different to you. You might find that you learn more from individuals that are different from you do than from people that you share interests with.

Focus on Learning More

Sometimes, you might think you know a person, but then, they start revealing stories and telling more parts of their life that alter your perspective on them. Always be open to learning more about certain individuals. You can never get to know someone enough, so don't limit yourself with what questions you might ask them or what conversation topics you choose to implement with that other person. You can learn more about the people that you spend every single day with. Even if you might think you know someone better than they know themselves, there's a good chance you still have more learning to do.

Learn How to Listen to Others

One of the biggest issues with communication is that we don't fully listen to others. We hear the words that they say, but we don't listen to what was meant behind that. This is a huge problem, especially when influencers might say something that gets published. Someone might say something that makes no sense out of context, but when put back into a conversation, it falls perfectly together.

Chapter 7: How Emotional Intelligence Affects Your Motivation

Emotional intelligence positively increases your ability to self-motivate, which leads to living a better life and growing your career more quickly: the self-awareness and emotional skills of people who have high EQ shine positive sunshine on their motor skills. Sometimes, when we've had little motivation for a long draw, it's hard to get motivated again, kind of like taking a cheat day that turns into a cheat week. We are merely human, so this is natural for us. We want more than we can quickly get, but we don't feel motivated to try hard to get what we want.

Motivated people set goals, and whenever they find themselves in crisis, they wonder why this is. Maybe the things happening in your life right now are making you too busy even to think you are positive. Or perhaps you don't get enough sleep. Either way, you can get out of that crisis. Setting a goal and achieving it is excellent. Goals help us focus our attention on the most important things, such as the ultimate goal. It's also easier to know for sure what you want when you focus on a single goal. Freelance motivation is pretty tricky, so make it easier by becoming a goal setter and a go-getter!

Motivated people also seek inspiration. One of the most significant impulses for anyone is something that truly inspires them deep inside. Look for someone who can be a good role model or idol and listen to the words they say. You can often find motivational speeches and inspiring stories easily on video streaming services. Emotional intelligence helps us get inspired because people with higher EQs are more profound thinkers. They can appreciate the beauty of things that others may not always see. You can find inspiration everywhere if you look for it and sincerely hope to find it. It's an incredibly positive trait to have to be able to locate inspiration wherever you are.

Be enthusiastic about achieving your goal. Do your best to feel and show enthusiasm. If someone tells you that they don't feel it or don't trust the process anymore, ask them to keep moving forward and be confident. As already mentioned, finding your inspiration can be the thrust inside you that makes you excited to wake up everyday and put on the coffee machine; excitement is a powerful emotion that makes us do things we never thought humanly possible. , because it makes our blood pump and our adrenaline flows through our bodies.

Anticipate the result. This might sound difficult, and many people just ignore it as if it didn't matter. But it works. Help people are struggling with nicotine addiction to quit smoking after many attempts. Help people cut alcohol out of their lives. Building the anticipation for the result is done by thinking about what it will be like after winning. If you find inspiration and want to start working towards one of your goals, don't start right away. Many of us will get excited and in a hurry and want to get started as soon as possible. This can be the end of it all, though. Set a future date and set it as the start date. Mark the calendar appropriately.

Create excitement for that date, then make it seem like it's the most important date of the month. Make your goal achievable and remind yourself of it every day. Maybe write it on a post-it and gum it on the fridge, or you could write it on a whiteboard. Either way, you should do your greatest to remind yourself of your goal every day. It may even benefit you to post your goal online on social media so your colleagues can help you hold yourself accountable. If you were trying to shed weight, maybe create a weight loss chart, put it on your bathroom door as long as you Think about your goal every day and ask for support. Perhaps talking about your goal will help you achieve it. You can always find someone who will support you, even on social media.

Realize that motivation isn't a steady stream of secure personal support. There may be an occasion when you find that your motivation is superficial. It comes and goes. This is one of the reasons why self-motivation is so important to you to be able to achieve. When you feel tired of your goals, or just plain weak and exhausted, there won't always be someone next to you with a bottle of water telling you to come back there. You have to be able to get on the plate and swing on your own sometimes. It's okay to get tired, and it's okay to want to quit, but it's not okay to let those feelings push your feet to the ground. Motivation won't make you feel like sunshine and rainbows all the time; it just helps you get started.

Stay faithful and never give up. If you have to halt, make sure you stop because you have to, not because you chose to. These are your goals. These are your dreams. Stick to them firmly, because life on this Earth is short, and you may not have another chance as good as the one you have. Don't be discouraged. You may not feel motivated today, and you may have to force yourself on and on your feet, but you better grit your teeth and stick. The motivation will return. It may come back a week or a month later, but it will come back. Your goal is a mile-long journey, and this little spot where you don't feel motivated is just a bump in the road. You have to walk this road like a wave across the ocean, facing all the ups and downs.

Now since we talked about all this emotion and the tsunami that can be, the discouragement may come from your goals being too big at first. It would be like saying: "my goal is to become a doctor." Without first starting with "I want to get my degree,". Start with smaller goals and achieve them individually. That way, you have a plan. However, don't allow yourself to get lazy and use your more modest goals as an excuse to work easier. You don't have to start by doing super intense workouts every day of the week; you can just start small and work until you do what's comfortable for you, but again, don't let these smaller goals be your excuse to refrain from pushing yourself.

Once you start building on these little successes, you will learn how rewarding they are. You can't fail if you start somewhere easy enough that you are sure to be successful. Once you've mastered that goal, hit the next one, then the future, and then keep chasing it. After a while, you will be able to look back on everything you have done and see how far it has taken you. Don't forget to share your successes with others as well. All of these positive things will help you learn how to motivate yourself. Not to mention, by taking small steps, you are far less likely to fail.

Now there is some time to take a break and read your goals. Look at the finished product often, as this will motivate you. Remind yourself to keep watching it and never forget why you started here. You started here because of that goal, so take a look at how to achieve it as hard as possible.

Also, maybe join an online forum or social media group to surround yourself with people who share similar goals to yours. These people are the ones who will help you get through those bumps on the road.

Thanks to them for that. You're going to need a fantastic support group, and those kinds of people most likely have a lot of experience where you lack them. Let them know that you are near or far from your goal and remember to ask for help. They may be telling you things you can't hear anywhere else, and they may have that vital hint that you never knew is an absolute game-changer.

So no, you're getting close to reaching your goal. Do your best not to stop and focus on the difficulties, focus on the reward you have coming for you in the end... This is a valuable piece of life that you should never let anyone take away from you. When you commit, you can do anything. You should aim high and work hard because one day you will wake up and be better than you.

Lastly, don't let negative thoughts prevail over positive ones due to lack of character. This isn't easy for anyone, and no matter how others have made it look, don't be fooled by the very particular parts of the process you have been shown. Everyone struggles with something, and everyone who has achieved your goal has probably worked their fingertips for it. Replace your negative thoughts with those and watch your motivation take off. There is no negativity when you can shed light on any situation because even failure can be seen as an opportunity to learn.

Chapter 8: Practical Exercises to Develop Emotional Intelligence

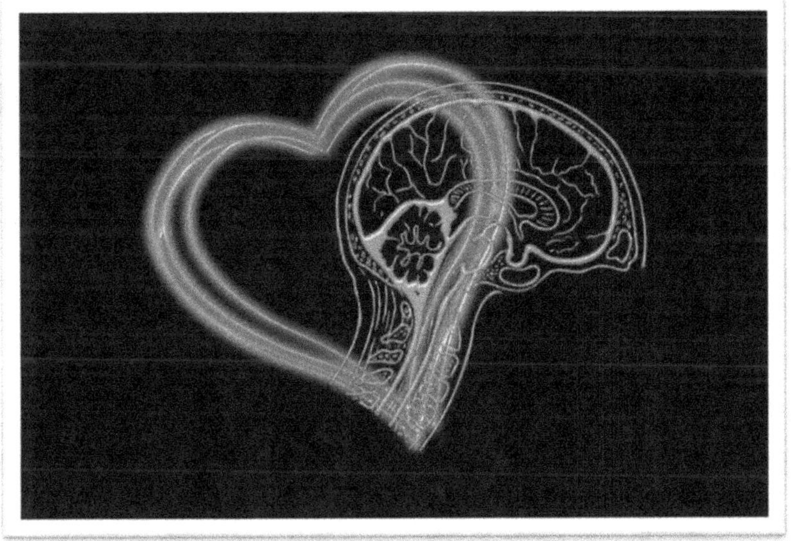

Think of your emotional intelligence as a muscle. To strengthen that muscle and build it up to where you want it to be, you need to exercise it consistently, just as you would with physical exercise.

Reflecting on Your Feelings

The first exercise that you can begin working to develop and improve your emotional intelligence is to begin by observing your feelings and reflecting on them. It is cool to fall out of reach with ourselves in this hectic world that we live in. From the moment we wake up each morning, our lives seem to be constantly on the go. Trying to manage one thing after another, taking care of ourselves often falls by the wayside, and we lose that connection to our innermost feelings. Instead of learning to focus on our emotions when they arise, we choose to do the easier, more convenient thing. We either brush it aside, ignore them, or deny them completely. Maybe even distract us from those feelings by doing something else. The more you deny your feelings, though, the harder it becomes to manage them later on. Bottling up your emotions and hoping they will just go away on its own has never proven to be an effective strategy. If it were, there wouldn't be quite so many people walking around lashing out emotionally or reacting impulsively. From now on, whenever you experience an emotion (no matter what it may be), observe it, acknowledge it, and reflect on how it is making you feel.

Make a Note of Your Triggers

This is something new because you've probably never done this before. Take your exercises towards building emotional intelligence one step further by writing down the triggers that cause you to become emotional each time you observe your feelings. What caused you to get worked up? What caused you to feel stressed? What's responsible for creating this feeling of happiness you now feel?

Whenever you make a note of every emotion you experience, write down, and make a list of the things that triggered it. Examine that list a couple of times a week. Do you notice any patterns? What is a recurring theme that you can spot? Understanding how to detect the triggers that cause extreme emotional reactions is key to learning how to manage your emotions. After all, you can't manage something that you don't know. You need to know what you're associating with before you can start making moves to remedy it.

Keep track of the emotional triggers!

Once you have found out the reasons behind the occurrence of every emotion, write down those reasons on your list. For instance, if there is a certain person or a certain event that invokes the emotion of anger in you, then you must write down this reason under the heading of anger.

Making use of those emotions

We must never underestimate how emotions affect our thoughts. Whenever we think about a certain thing, our emotions control our reactions to that thing.

Emotions don't just tend to occur on a sudden basis. They occur due to reasons that have been supporting them for a certain period. For instance, you are getting late in the morning while driving to work. You see a car with a busted tire standing during the road. You start angrily shouting at the driver of that car to move his car away from the road. This anger didn't just occur as a sudden reaction to the flat tire of that car, but it occurred because you woke up late that morning due to which you were already late for your work.

At the end comes the task of managing your emotions. For some people, this task is known to be the biggest challenge in their life. Managing your emotions is not just a one-day task, but it requires a continuous struggle. However, once you master this task, managing your emotions might become the easiest thing on this planet.

Take a Timeout When You Need It

An emotionally intelligent person does not let their feelings overwhelm them. They always remain cool, calm, and collected. They always respond appropriately. More importantly, they know when to take time out and return to the situation with a better solution. It is easy to let your feelings overwhelm you if you're not careful.

As much as you want to resolve the conflict there and then, sometimes, you need to take a time-out or a five-minute breather just to clear your head whenever your emotions are starting to get the best of you. That is the intelligent thing to do.

Start Practicing Responding

Where before this, you may have been more prone to reacting impulsively each time you had an extreme emotional reaction, now you need to adopt a new exercise. You need to learn how to respond first instead of reacting. You now need to respond to your first default mode, and you do that with self-awareness and self-regulation. By giving attention to your emotions, especially those that trigger an extreme reaction in the past, you can then learn how to regulate yourself. You can make a conscious effort to choose the next move you will make instead of letting your emotions drive you. You will do the intelligent thing by leading with your head, not your heart. This is why it is important to emulate the steps above, especially learning how to identify your triggers. If you know, something will trigger an extreme emotional response, take measures to that put a stop to that through self-regulation.

No Room for Superiority

An emotionally intelligent person is that way because of one thing – they are humble. It simply won't do without thinking that you may be better than everyone, or that someone is not on par with you, which makes you more superior. You will never achieve a leadership position if you inflict an air of superiority because no one will ever respect a leader who makes it difficult to be likable. When you choose not to be humble, you make it very difficult to achieve self-awareness because you will be blinded to your faults. It's no problem for you to point out the flaws in others immediately, but you won't be able to note the things that you are doing wrong. See everyone as an equal, not a subordinate. No matter what family they come from, everyone deserves to be treated respectfully. Display emotional intelligence by always choosing to be humble, approachable, likable, and pleasant.

Avoid Overthinking

One of the reasons that we sometimes become more emotional than we should is because we tend to overthink a lot of things. A simple matter which could be resolved easily could potentially get blown out of proportion because someone was reacting to it in a highly emotional way. To start exercising better emotional intelligence on your part, what you could do is to stop overthinking situations and just see things for what they are. You do that by looking at the facts in front of you. If something is not a fact, then don't think about it. Observe the situation in front of you and see things as they are. Don't embellish, don't assume, and don't add on facts of your own. This is how things get more complicated than they should, and emotions get fired up when there was no need to be.

Writing Down Your Feelings

Bring paper and a pen. Note down the emotions that you feel regularly. Point out your physical reactions to each type of emotion under the heading of that emotion. For instance, you have written down the emotion of HURT, which you feel now and then. Whether you cry or feel a sense of loss, just write it down on your list. Once you have completed the first emotion and its symptoms, move on towards the next emotion.

Pour your heart out, open the floodgates of emotion, and just let it flow until you're done. When you've finished, read what you've just written down. Assess your thoughts, observe how you're feeling and reflect upon why and what triggered such emotion within you. Once you've finished and felt better, you can always tear up or shred the paper. Do you notice how you sometimes feel better after talking about your feelings with someone? It works the same way, except that by writing it down, you ensure that you always have an outlet for your emotions, even when no one is available.

Chapter 9: Practical Ways to Be Happy and Enjoy Life

We have looked at emotions, the process of formation of emotions, and the cause of emotions. We have also dealt with negativity, the causes of negativity, consequences, and how to deal with negativity. We have observed the relationship between negativity and emotions and how negativity affects our emotions. The manifestation of our emotions is linked with negative thoughts and positive thoughts in our lives. If you want to attain full reprogramming of your brain, you must get the interconnection between all these factors.

You must be able to examine your emotions and see the cause of your emotions. You must be in a position to scrutinize your behavior and reaction to emotional provocation to determine if you are affected by negativity or not. You also need to look at your life to see if there are any signs and symptoms of negativity such as overthinking, hatred, and so on.

Although life is full of hardships and disappointments, circumstances should never stop you from living a happy life. A happy life is full of joy and contentment. When a person is happy with their life, they do not complain. Happiness is brought about by contentment, love, and understanding. If you want to be happy and enjoy life, you must find a way of addressing all the negativity in your heart and your mind. You need to find a way of healing wounds inflicted by abuse and failure. You need to find a way of rising above your fears and weaknesses. Happiness is brought about by understanding that you are not perfect, but you are good enough. People may make you feel like you are not good enough for the world.

The truth is that everybody is good enough for the word.

No matter your weakness and disabilities, there is something important you contribute to the world. Your words alone are good enough to change the world. Your way of life alone should be good enough to influence people and make the world a better place. Once you recognize your strengths and abilities, you step into space where you can influence the world. You move from self-pity, low self-esteem, and negativity. You move to a space of positivity, progress, and success.

To help you get out of any negativity and focus on positivity, we will employ several therapeutic techniques such as meditation to help you come back to your original personality.

What Is Meditation?

Meditation is the process of training your mind to focus and redirect from negative thoughts to positive thoughts. Many meditation techniques can be used to reach different levels of mind control. The entire process of reprogramming your mind is in some way linked to meditation.

To understand meditation, think of yourself as a car. Your mind is the engine, and your free will is the steering wheel. When a car is moving, it obeys all the commands given to it by the steering wheel. If the steering wheel turns to the left, the car has to turn to the left. If you step on the gas and allow the car to speed off without controlling the steering wheel, the car will move on in a straight stretch, probably a straight road for a while until it comes to a corner. In this instance, the car will continue moving in the straight line and eventually bump into a bush or a wall. The same case applies to our minds. The mind is just an engine for your life. However, you have something greater than the mind; that is the free will. Your free will is used to decide which side to go. Your free will is the driver in your car. The brain may be the engine of your body, but it does not know where the right direction is. The free-will chooses to either listen to your mind, your heart, or your flesh.

Meditation is the process of redirecting your brain. It is the process of controlling the engine to ensure that the rest of the car moves in the right direction. Although all processes start from the engine, the engine does not have control over the car. The engine does not know where a car should be going except forward. In our example, you realize that the car will keep pushing in a certain direction, even if it leads to a bush. Your free will has to decide where the mind should be focused on. This is the reason why your brain is often caught in negativity.

When you travel on the straight path of life, your brain does not know what direction is right or wrong. Your brain accepts the signals given to it by people and life circumstances. Your brain records the signals that say you are unable to do this and that. Your brain will forever remember the failures that you went through. On this straight path of life, the brain does not know the difference between lies and truth. It is the inner part of you that can make a choice; to choose between good and bad and differentiate between positivity and negativity.

There are many positive benefits of meditation. Getting to understand the benefits one by one will help you appreciate the beauty of meditation

What Is Mindfulness?

Mindfulness is a meditation technique that focuses on self-awareness. Self-awareness is the ability to determine your feelings, thoughts, and behavior. Without self-awareness, no one can change their behavior or character. Self-awareness calls for a constant examination of personal actions.

During mindfulness meditation, a person may choose to focus their mind on any part of their body. You may choose to focus your thoughts on your legs or any other part of your body. For instance, you may choose to focus your mind on your leg, feel the temperature, the hairs, movement of wind, blood flow, and the entire environment around your leg. Through this type of meditation, you can capture areas of pain within the body and slowly release it out through breath and or imagination. Meditation is a complex process that leads to the healing of wounds, both physical and emotional. It is believed that medication often results in chemical changes in the body and the mind. These changes foster quick recovery for wounds and help release pain.

Practice Mindfulness

Practicing mindfulness is one of the most effective techniques for healing old wounds. It is also effective in removing negative energy and reducing the effects of negativity. If you have been suffering from the effects of negativity such as overthinking, depression, anxiety, and so on, you can turn your life around by practicing mindfulness.

As mentioned, mindfulness entails paying attention to your body, your thoughts, and your feelings. It is the first step to self-awareness. If you want to attain the full reprogramming of your life, you must start by gaining awareness. Awareness means that you are alert to everything that happens within you and around you. This is not something you can attain easily. Our minds are often focused on life. We always want to chase the next dollar and take little time to notice our feelings or actions. To start gaining any perspective into the matters of personal emotion, we must come to a place where we have a perspective of the things that happen around us.

Practicing mindfulness opens the doors to self-awareness. Practicing mindfulness for 30 minutes in a day will help you start understanding yourself. You start visualizing your thoughts and feelings. It is during meditation that you realize you are angry or sad. During meditation, you can tell your moods and emotion. Negative emotions within your mind must be addressed if you want to move on with your life in a positive direction. This is the first step to spotting any negative energy. You also get to spot any effects of negativity in your life. You start realizing that you are afraid of something or someone.

Through meditation, you detect the areas of pain in your body and start observing your feelings objectively.

Practicing mindfulness takes you to a safe spot where your mind enjoys unsearchable peace. The beauty of this type of meditation is that it does not involve judgment. When practicing mindfulness, everything is deemed right. You are not supposed to judge yourself for the things you like or desire. When you are in your safe place, everything is right. You are allowed to admire and covet things that would be termed socially contrary without judging yourself. You are allowed to be your true self. As we stated in the beginning, our minds are only restricted by what we know. Reprogramming your brain entails changing what you have been made to believe is the truth. The reality of the matter is that you are free to do whatever you want. You should not let people's thoughts or opinions hold your life down.

The words of judgment from men and society often discourage people from pursuing happiness in life. However, discovering that nothing is stopping you from being happy gives you the freedom to open your mind up for new opportunities.

Most people work hard in school, intending to get a good job. This is something that has been instilled in our minds by society. We have been made to believe that to live a good life, and we must be the best in school. When a person fails to succeed in academics, they are most likely to lose focus in life and feel dejected. Many times, you will find that people struggle to excel in areas where they are not good, or they do not even enjoy just to please society.

Chapter 10: Applications of Emotional Intelligence

Understanding how EQ can affect various aspects of relationships is key to seeing how deeply it can impact your life. This section will provide what a high EQ looks like in each of the following situations and compare it to what might happen when someone with a lower EQ is also in the same location. The difference between the two can be astounding when compared side by side.

EQ in romantic relationships

Imagine that you and your spouse are arguing again. Your spouse is a stay-at-home parent for young children as you work full time during standard office hours. Every day you come home, your spouse asks for help as soon as you walk in the door. You can see your spouse looking stressed out, still wearing dirty pajamas, dinner is on the stove, cooking, and the living room looks like a toy bomb exploded. The kids are arguing, and your spouse quickly pushes the kids towards you and hands you the spatula before disappearing into the bathroom, closing and closing the door, and opening the shower.

Assuming you have a lower EQ, you may immediately get angry. After all, you have just come home from work and are mentally drained from a working day in the office. Your spouse has to stay home, you tell yourself angrily, and it seems like your spouse hasn't done anything all day. The house is destroyed, the children are not fed, and the dinner is not over. In your anger, you follow your spouse to the bathroom and proceed to scream through the door. You don't recognize that your spouse seemed stressed before leaving, or you think that all your spouse had heard all day was the sound of kids' bickering that was escalating your anger. Babies listen to you scream from the door and run away crying. Your spouse does not open the door. Dinner burns on the stove. All of this aggravates your anger and makes the situation worse. Your relationships with both your spouse and your children have been damaged. Your spouse feels like you are not supportive, and your children learn to avoid you because you are an angry person.

Stop and think about how the situation would have turned out if you had had a higher EQ. You would walk in the door and see the despair painted on your spouse's face. You would have been able to feel the stress and anxiety practically coming from your spouse and see how overwhelmed your spouse was with the situation. Instead of getting angry, you would have seen that what your spouse needed was a quick respite from the constant annoyance of children. You would have happily entertained the children, and the change of pace may have been enough to stop their disputes. You would have finished dinner, serving it up and serving the children, who ran happily to eat. Your spouse would have come out of the shower feeling much more comfortable and ready to face the rest of the evening, and you would have felt supported and loved because you took the initiative to relieve some stress. Your relationship, instead of being hurt, was strengthened by your ability to scale the situation. Also, your children learn that marriage is a partnership. The random comparison is harmful, and what a marriage needs is for both partners to take care of each other's needs, even when they are not verbally expressed and even when they may not be convenient.

EQ in family relationships

Imagine that your children have been misbehaving all day. They keep running around the house like children do when locked up in the house due to bad weather, and no matter how often you tell them to stop, you can hear the sound of their quick footsteps running down the hall again a few minutes later. After reminding them to stay for the umpteenth time and enjoy the momentary relief from the constant blows of the feet, their rush is heard starting again, followed by a loud bang and the glass shattering. Run outside and see that your kids, because they weren't listening, ran into the hutch and knocked out a whole row of wine glasses, which shattered all over the floor.

Assuming you have low EQ, chances are you wind up and scream. You immediately yell at the children for not listening to them, chewing on them for the disobedience that ruined everything, and telling them to look at the mess they left you. Despite the fear, pain, and guilt on their faces, you belittle them for not listening, say something along the lines of accusing them of not being good guys or wishing they weren't there, and yelling at both of them to go to theirs. Rooms for the rest of the night. Your children stare at you in horror for a moment before bursting into tears and running away. You ignored the fact that one of the kids had a cut in their foot, and the other was terrified of you, and you ignored the damage your outburst has had on your kids.

With a higher EQ, you would have run out to see what happened and immediately ask if your kids are okay. You would go through them, grab each of them from the glass and take them to the other room to patch them up while you had a serious but still calm conversation about why you asked them not to play so brutally indoors. Instead of losing your temper, you used the accident to teach the children a lesson. When they were all patched up, you brought them back to clutter and asked them to help you clean it up in an age-appropriate way. Each child contributed to the chaos, and each of them sincerely apologized. You hugged your kids, reminded them that you love them, and sternly told them to avoid running around the house. They nodded and went off to play alone, feeling secure in their attachment to you, and having learned a precious lesson. You have strengthened your relationship with your children, and they have learned that they can count on you in times of need, thanks to your balanced response to what used to be a messy situation.

EQ in platonic relationships

Imagine getting ready to have your friend come over to your house for an evening of video games, a few beers, and some pizza. It's a low-key event meant to be relaxing. The time your friend was supposed to arrive came and went, and almost an hour later, he finally shows up. He seems upset about something and mumbles apologies, but completely avoids the subject of why he was late. Instead, he grabs a beer, sits quietly, and watches you play. He drinks the beer and then takes another without saying a word. He turns the phone off and on again, his expression darkening every time he does.

If you have a lower EQ, you may respond negatively. You're hurt that your friend was late and didn't offer an apology or explanation. You are angry because you feel devalued. You're sad that your friend doesn't seem to care that you feel upset about his actions. Instead of looking at him and seeing his feelings, you look at him and snap. You tell him that if he doesn't want to be there, and it seems like he is, then he can just walk away because you don't need his negativity to lower the mood when you wanted to have fun. You scold him for checking his phone so often and tell him he's a bad friend, and you refuse to put up with such disrespect. In response, your friend doesn't say a word. He picks up the phone, looks like he might cry, and walks away. He texts you again, never responds when you call and refuses to recognize you every time you see him around. He ended the friendship for your outburst.

With a higher EQ, you may have looked at the situation and seen that your friend was not doing well. At first glance, you would have been able to see the pain in his expression upon entering your door and would have been more willing to provide him with the support he needed. Despite the annoyance you felt, you also realized that your friend was unwell, which replaced your annoyance. Even if he didn't want to talk about what had happened, you would have seen that what he needed right now was to be supported during some sort of personal struggle. Instead of putting it down, you would have patiently waited for him to share what happened, and while you expected, you would have continued to play and genuinely enjoy your friend's company. Finally,

EQ in workplace relationships

Imagine you are at work. You have a group project that you and your colleagues have been working on in the last month. The day before the project presentation, you all realize that no one has worked on a specific part of the project that was incredibly important, and without it, your project cannot be presented. Each of you thought another person would complete that part of the project, and no one checked it until the day before the deadline when you were putting the project together to review the final project. The last piece of the project takes a long time.

With lower EQ, you could explode on your peers. You can shout that it's not done and blame other people around you, looking for any explanation that removes the blame from yourself. You say it was your colleague Mary's fault because she should have done something related to it. You may yell out some words that aren't appropriate in the workplace and get you in trouble with HR. The assignment is never carried out. Also, you are all reprimanded for failing to meet the requirements and find yourself without a job due to the situation escalating so severely.

With a higher EQ, you may be angry, and you may have seen the frustration on everyone else's faces, but instead of giving in to that anger and frustration, you've chosen to analyze the situation instead. You've looked at what was still needed, and while it would be a lot for a single person to complete, point out that it's something you can all finish relatively quickly if everyone takes a portion of it. Everyone in your group looks to you to listen to you, and soon the mood seems to calm down. Your colleagues follow your lead, and within a few hours, you have completed the remaining work together. Your project is submitted on time, and everyone is thrilled with the result. You feel happy and satisfied because you managed to turn a bad situation into a good one, and your colleagues feel like you are trustworthy and like they can count on you when things get tough. The next time you all have a project, you are appointed the leader responsible for making sure everyone has a role, and everything is completed. This newfound admiration from peers improves your reputation with your bosses, and you soon find yourself with a raise and promotion thanks to your tact and emotional intelligence.

Chapter 11: Dealing with a Partner Who Has Low Emotional

Intelligence

Watch your tone

Some people score poorly in EQ not because they want to but because they do not know better. Your role as an emotionally intelligent partner or spouse is to bring your partner to the other side. The side where people speak respectfully and with empathy. The side where people are good listeners who do not interrupt others while they are talking. Being condescending about your superior emotional intelligence will only make your partner resentful of you.

Be realistic about your expectations

You've been suspecting that your partner has low EQ all along, and this book has cemented this suspicion by providing you with solid evidence of what EQ is and what it is not. Now what? Should you share this book with your partner and demand that they read it from cover to cover and report back to you in a week, complete with a higher EQ?

Your partner might not even be up for it. They might fight you when you suggest that they should try doing this or that. Remember that low EQ people tend to hate change. Converting your partner will not be a walk in the park. However, if your partner truly loves you and is committed to your relationship, then you can help them get started on the baby steps that they need to take for the relationship to become even more fulfilling than it is.

Remember its okay to fight

Every relationship has its fights. There can never be a relationship without fights unless the parties are afraid to share their true opinions. Fights strengthen relationships. They give a platform for partners to share the feelings that they have kept hidden deep within. Whether you are fighting about EQ-related matters or any other thing, do not feel any guilt or shame over it. Even the most emotionally intelligent people fight with their loved ones. They just know better than to yell or name-call or hit. As long as you are fighting without tearing each other down, you are on the right track.

Let the other person choose to change

You can indeed influence another person into changing by modeling the kind of behavior that is appropriate. However, you can never force a person that does not want to change to change. Change is such a personal decision that must be made by an individual when they are ready for it. If your spouse behaves in a particular manner that you find to be emotionally immature, they have to get to a place where they see it from your perspective, and then decide to change. This might take a whole lot of time and may even seem impossible at first. Sitting around, waiting for them to be ready might take up all your patience. Only you will be in a position to decide whether they are worth the wait or not.

Sometimes you'll have to walk away

At some point, you have to pull the plug on a relationship that is not working. Relationships are not recyclable plastics that you can keep and use for another purpose when you are done using them for what they were originally intended. A relationship is supposed to be positive addition in your life. If your partner is exhibiting signs of low or nonexistent emotional intelligence, including being emotionally abusive, it is well within your right to walk away. You should not only walk but run as fast as your high EQ heels can carry you. Somewhere out, there is someone who is self-aware and motivated that is bound to appreciate a respectful relationship with an emotionally mature adult such as yourself.

Strategies to Improve and Rescue Relationships in Both Your Work and Personal Life

Acknowledge and Celebrate Differences

Nonetheless, you must steer away from such ideologies. You might be different but get it clear that the world would have been a boring place if we were the same. As such, accept differences and learn to celebrate them.

Listen Effectively

There is power in listening to what other people have to say. Psychologists argue that listening is a silent type of flattery. By actively listening, you give people the impression that they are valued. You are giving them time to express themselves without interfering. With regards to creating meaningful relationships, listening stands as a fundamental thing that you ought to do.

You must realize that you shouldn't just listen, but you should actively listen to what folks have to say. There is a difference here. Actively listening implies that you listen while also showing concern. Remember, it is important to express your understanding of what the other party is feeling or desiring. After knowing what they want, you can move on to respond.

Give People Time

It is impossible to create meaningful connections with people without giving them your time. Giving people time is a special gift. Usually, we often claim that we don't have time. Therefore, by offering to spend time with friends, family, and colleagues, it means a lot. There is a lot that you will be sacrificing when you spend your precious time with individuals you care about. In the end, you find yourself developing strong bonds with those you interact with. Unfortunately, the advent of technology has made it impossible to create beneficial relationships. Today, most people will plan for a gathering where they get to spend most of their time on their phones. This means that their presence is not felt. Technological devices have robbed people of the value that they would have generated when others create time for them. Consequently, part of ensuring that you give people the time they need, you also need to make yourself present; mentally and physically.

Improve Your Communication Skills

Communication is yet another key factor that will confirm that you create purposeful relations with people. A huge challenge experienced by most people in communication is that they make assumptions. Often, some folks tend to think that others have understood them. Making assumptions leads to misunderstandings, and this negatively affects how people relate. At work, failing to communicate effectively could lead to backstabbing and blaming each other.

Good communication at work will have a positive impact on the overall morale of workers. In this case, when a leader conveys information clearly, junior workers will find it easy to follow instructions. Synergy will also be felt if at all people are working in groups.

Poor communication will also affect love affairs. Without understanding what your partner needs, there is a likelihood that things will fall apart. Successful relationships dwell on communication. Partners who always listen to each other will find ways of solving their issues amicably.

Manage Mobile Technology

The importance of managing how you use your devices is worth repeating over and over again. Most relationships have suffered because people don't know how to use their devices. In social gatherings, it is not surprising to find people glued to their mobile phones. Undeniably, this is not the best way of interacting with people. Sure, the use of mobile technology has transformed the way we communicate. However, the bitter truth is that it is negatively affecting our relationships. Consequently, something must be done. Change begins with you; learn how to use your mobile handset wisely.

Feedback

Communication will not be complete without providing feedback to those you are relating with. To create beneficial relationships, you must provide others with constructive feedback. Don't just respond without stopping for a moment to think. You want to evaluate whether what you were about to say is pertinent. About to say is important. Other people will value positive feedback from your end. This is an essential ingredient in building a strong connection with those around you.

There is always something to gain in the relationships we enter into. Having a positive outlook on any engagement you enter into will have a lasting impact. The best part is that you will live a happier life surrounded by people you love.

Chapter 12: Managing Your Emotions

Understanding Your Emotions

It is not uncommon for people to think that negative emotions are bad, indicating that a person is inherently bad. It is okay to want to feel good most of the time, but that does not suggest that you feel sorry for how you feel. Do not assume that you are bad because you feel terrible or that someone else is better than you because they feel good. Feelings are just what they are, and you cannot control how you feel, neither should you try.

Allow the feelings to do what they are naturally designed to do, conveying information to you. Your job is to focus on how to control your responses to how you feel. In other words, how you behave when you feel a certain way is under your direct control. It might not seem that way to you if you think that triggers, emotions, feelings, and reactions happen simultaneously. But they don't, and that's a good thing because that gives you enough time to take charge of your responses. I suggest you quit beating up on yourself for feeling bad. Instead, be grateful for recognizing a bad feeling because that is your cue to carefully consider your response before reacting to the emotions you are feeling.

To fully understand the purpose of your emotions, it is important to understand what your emotions are.

Emotions are electrochemical signals in your body that are released in response to how you perceive your world. In other words, your perception of the world (good or bad) determines what signals are released in your body. Your emotions are indications of your interpretation or perception of events in and around you.

Although all emotions don't feel the same, they are essentially neutral. That is, they are neither good nor bad. Some may feel good while others feel bad, but the feelings are important information that tells you to keep going or tread carefully. Do you now see that suppressing an emotion doesn't serve you well? Instead of stifling an emotion, listen to its message, and choose your response.

Every emotion has a corresponding message. But you will miss the message if you have not trained yourself to listen for it. Below are four different charts that list different emotions and messages. Study them to get a clue into what your emotions are telling you. The messages may vary depending on the individual and their core beliefs, but the chart gives you a general idea of what each emotion represents.

Getting a Handle on Your Emotions

So what do you do if you are feeling bad and you are not supposed to suppress your emotions? First of all, understand that suppressing your emotions is not true self-regulation or management. Even if your intentions are good, when you suppress your feelings, it can lead to resentment in relationships, insincerity, more negative feelings, and high blood pressure if you keep it up over a long period.

However, expressing or acting on your emotions the way you feel them can be disastrous too. The goal of improving your emotional intelligence will be defeated if you continue to act on your emotions because you don't want to suppress them. Your best approach would be to reappraise your emotions.

Reappraising your emotions means seeking alternative interpretations for a challenging situation. True self-management involves embracing changes. If something goes against your beliefs, your emotions will trigger a feeling response to alert you of the contradiction. But if you expand your view to include new beliefs, your emotions will morph according to the new set of beliefs. This is why you must be willing to look at things from other perspectives while staying true to your core values.

To effectively reappraise a situation, you must necessarily suspend your disbelief. For example, your partner failed to keep their promise, and you feel really bad. Picking a fight with them will not make them feel good; neither will it change the situation. On the other hand, ignoring how you feel and wearing a limp smile doesn't improve your mood, either. When you reappraise the situation, you will start to think along the lines of:

"They may have failed me, but I'm sure they are not failures themselves."

"I can't make them do what they are unwilling to do. Perhaps, I am expecting too much from them."

"Perhaps they didn't mean to hurt me or fail in keeping their promises. I have made mistakes in time past too."

Thinking this way will broaden your horizons and allow you to embrace other possibilities. With that understanding will come a relief from whatever negative emotions you may have felt previously. And in that clear space, you are in a better place to make sound decisions you won't regret later.

Here are two quick, simple, but effective exercises to help you get a handle on your emotions.

1.   When you are in a situation that has your emotions running wild, deliberately reduce your heart rate by shortening your inhales

and prolonging your exhales. This will effectively reduce your blood pressure and the urge to react immediately.

2.   Think of the situation as a challenge instead of a threat. Taking on a challenge is more motivating than facing a threat. Usually, you would avoid a threat but seek ways to overcome a challenge.

It is important always to remember that there is no need to rush into reacting if there is no immediate danger. If you can keep your emotions under check, you will be able to handle situations rationally regardless of how challenging they may appear to be at first.

Practical Tips For Controlling Your Reactions to Your Emotions

•   Acknowledge your emotions. Don't ignore them because the more you do that, the more intense the emotion gets. Acknowledge your emotions by naming them. For example, "I am feeling annoyed!" Acknowledging your emotions lessens their intensity and grip on you.

•   Let go of worry, especially when there is nothing you can do about a situation. Instead of fretting about a situation, focus on what you can control and do something about them. Worry only serves to increase your stress level.

•	Consider feedback before internalizing it. If someone gave you a new shirt, you wouldn't throw it over your head and rush to an important meeting. You would first put it on to make sure that it fits and that you like it, and then you would decide if it is suitable for your important meeting. That is how you should approach feedback. When someone says something about you, take a moment to see if it fits instead of internalizing and reacting immediately.

•	Expand your horizon. Don't wait until emotions are high before you try to seek other perspectives. Learn about other people's beliefs and values. See where you can shift grounds if necessary without losing yourself. Doing this regularly, especially when you relate with people from different backgrounds, will forestall possible conflict of values. Also, realize that events don't have any inherent meanings besides the ones you give them. Feeling emotionally hurt is usually as a result of interpreting something differently. Try to soften your interpretations where necessary to minimize getting hurt.

•	Realize that it is okay to feel bad sometimes. Give yourself enough time to process negative emotions. If you feel sad, disappointed, or angry, it is okay to feel those feelings. But don't let them derail you from normal functioning. If you don't allow yourself to process these feelings, they will explode when you least expect.

Using the EQ-i 2.0 Tool

Emotional quotient (EQ) is the measurement of a person's knowledge of how emotions work. EQ levels are determined through test scores. But unless you can demonstrate your EQ skills in real-life situations, having a high score in an EQ test is pretty much useless.

A high EQ score is particularly useful in work relationships or team situations where organizations measure an individual's emotional intelligence level using EQ tests. One such test instrument is the Emotional Quotient Inventory (EQ-i 2.0). The "2.0" stands for the second generation. It is an updated version of the EQ-i tool.

EQ-i 2.0 is the first scientifically proven instrument for measuring emotional intelligence. For more than 20 years, the EQ-i 2.0 tool has been used by millions of people worldwide. It is a self-report tool that appraises an individual's emotional and social functioning, particularly in the workplace. The instrument uses 133 questions to measure a person's skills in different areas, including adaptability, stress management, interpersonal, intrapersonal, and general mood.

The image below is a model of the EQ-i 2.0 tool. It shows how behavior can be predicted using 5 composite scales and 15 subscales.

The model's circular nature demonstrates how one aspect of emotional intelligence blends into another.

If you are particular about improving your workplace relationships, I highly recommend this tool. It will help you focus on your areas of excellence and get the most out of your daily activities. The tool is not an end in itself, but a starting point for your work toward better job performance and great working relationships.

Chapter 13: Understanding Emotional Drain and Energy Vampires

Up until this point, we have made one significant assumption in this book: that you are surrounded by emotionally mature and decent people in your life who are solely motivated by the desire to take advantage of you. The nature of emotional intelligence, especially the empathy component, is such that you will be giving a whole lot of you to others. You will be investing your emotions to gain an understanding of other people's feelings. You will also be investing your time in trying to appreciate other people's thoughts. What happens when you start to feel drained? What causes you to start feeling drained in the first place?

Have you ever spent some time with someone only to leave their company feeling extremely drained? Or maybe you have dated a partner who seemed to enjoy leaving you depleted of all your emotional resources. It might also be that you work with colleagues that leave you feeling worse for wear at the end of every workday. The emotional drain manifests itself in various ways. It is the effect of being under too much stress, both mentally and emotionally. The emotional drain might look like boredom, irritation, sadness, and even anxiety. Whatever it may look like, emotional drain is a very serious problem. Going through long periods of emotional drain sometimes has tragic consequences in the end.

Signs of Emotional Drain

Besides feeling exhausted after an interaction with someone, numerous other signs can point to a problem. Unfortunately, many of these signs can be attributed to other things, which explains why they might go unnoticed for a long time. For instance, if you are having trouble sleeping, you might think it is stressed about tomorrow's presentation. The real cause might be that you are in an emotionally draining relationship with an energy vampire, which brings us to the first sign of emotional drain: insomnia.

Insomnia

You'd think that the brain would know to fall asleep when you are emotionally depleted to allow you the chance for some required rest, but this is not the case. The emotional drain is often accompanied by stress, characterized by a racing mind that is trying to contain a million and one thoughts. When your mind is in this state, it can be very difficult to quiet down for a night of relaxing sleep. If you have trouble sleeping and have not undergone a major life event that would explain your insomnia, you might want to look around at the people you spend your time with. One of them might be sapping all the joy and life from you, leaving you with nothing to look forward to at the end of the night.

Lack of Motivation

We said that motivation is the force behind the go-getter attitude that allows us to achieve our long-term goals, even if it means putting up with the hard work of the present. To be a highly motivated individual, you must be at a good place mentally.

When you are down in the dumps, you lack the necessary emotional resources to motivate yourself. The things you used to love are no longer appealing, and you have to give yourself a pep talk before getting out of bed in the morning. Energy vampires have a way of stealing all the resources from you.

An energy vampire might come in the form of a boss who is always criticizing your work unfairly, even when you have delivered pure gold. You will likely not have the mental or emotional energy to get into it with such a boss or even the job itself after several months of constant criticism. While you had previously enjoyed your job, you will likely catch yourself,, not wanting to show up at the office.

Hopelessness

Hope is a thing that has been channeled by many a person to get themselves through difficult situations in life. When a person is without hope, they see no end to their suffering. They believe that what they are going through is permanent and that every day they live through will be worse than the previous. Hope is powerful, and the absence of it is also powerful, albeit with the opposite effect. Martin Luther King, Jr., said this about hope: *Everything that is done in this world is done by hope.* So how can you expect to do anything when you have no hope?

Energy vampires who are intentional in their emotional abuse are especially good at sucking out all the hope from your life. A narcissist, for instance, might make you feel as if you are the most worthless person in the world and that you'll never be able to achieve anything. When you get such a review from a person that you love, it is easy to lose any hope that you had for the future.

How to Deal with Energy Vampires

As noted, energy vampires are all around us. You can also be an energy vampire depending on the circumstances in your life. For instance, there are times in your life when you might be extremely needy and codependent, depending on what you are going through. If you have ever needed someone to fill a space or need in your life, you probably were an energy vampire at that moment.

Seeing that we all can be energy vampires, is there any need to learn how to deal with it? Would it not be easier just to let ourselves exist in our natural states as well-meaning but somewhat needy people who sometimes suck the soul out of others without intending to? Unfortunately, there are those vampires that will leave a trail of emotionally drained people in their wake without feeling any bit of remorse about it. An energy vampire of that kind can do a whole lot of destruction, which is why it is important to know how to deal with the intentional and calculating emotional vampire.

The very first thing that you need to do when dealing with an energy vampire is to recognize them for who they are. Often, we are involved with the wrong people for a long period before realizing what exactly they are and the damage they cause in our lives. If the feeling you get after spending time with someone is constantly negative, consider this a red flag that you want. As human beings, we tend to extend a whole lot of grace and forgiveness to people who do not deserve any of those things.

You will need to learn when dealing with energy vampires is how to ground yourself. Grounding yourself involves knowing who you are, understanding yourself, and remaining true to who you are so that you are not easily swayed by people who come in and out of your life. You must have a clear and solid understanding of your individuality and your energy. Energy vampires have a way of identifying vulnerable people that they can take advantage of. Vulnerable people include those who are easily influenced. For example, if you are easily rattled by what people think and say about you, you will become the perfect fodder for emotional vampires.

Types of Energy Vampire

Finally, it is important to note that energy vampires come in different shapes and sizes. While they all have the same result of draining someone of their energy, they implement their devious ways differently. Here are the noteworthy energy vampires that you should be on the lookout for:

The Forever Victim

Some people just love being the victim in every story. They play the role perfectly and use every opportunity to let the world know how unfair life is to them. If you have such a person in your life, you will quickly get tired of hearing them whine about everything and anything. They whine when the boss requires that they do the job they were hired to do. They complain when they face a minor inconvenience. They complain when you do not pick their calls because you were at a meeting, and they'll even complain after you pick up their call because they think your tone is harsh or unfriendly, or whatever they want it to be for that occasion. If you think reading about the things a person with a victim mentality will complain about makes you feel exhausted, imagine what the actual complaining does to a person who has to deal with such an energy vampire. It can be truly energy-depleting. Long after you have left the company of such an energy vampire, you will still hear their whiny little voice ringing in your ears.

The It's-All-About-Me Vampire AKA the Narcissist

Imagine living your life with someone who does not consider you a person worthy of empathy or any other sort of consideration. This is what a narcissistic energy vampire is all about. To them, the world revolves around them. If they sneeze, you must run immediately to them and see if they are about to catch a cold. God forbid that is the case because now you have to shelve your life and ensure they recover by administering tender, loving care that they would not be willing to spare if the roles were reversed. A narcissist vampire will make you feel as if you were born to do their bidding. They will steal all your sense of empowerment and leave you feeling deflated and worse for wear. Even when they sense you are getting overwhelmed, such vampires never quit. They take and take and take until there is nothing left of you to take.

The Intimidator

It is a matter of the fact that weakness is louder than strength; the Intimidator is an energy vampire that is lacking in strength. As such, they compensate by trying to act tough and strong when, in fact, they are quivering in their boots beneath the surface. The Intimidator is an emotional vampire that likes to dominate every space they are in, regardless of the circumstances or the occasion. They talk the loudest in the room, are often inappropriate, like to push people around, and will have no hesitation spewing hate when they know they can hide being something. You will often find many intimidators hiding behind computer screens and spewing their hate and bigotry about everything and anything. Intimidators often find strength in numbers (of their kind) because they know they lack the innate strength to act alone. Intimidators do not care for other people's points of view. Only their opinions matter. An energy vampire of the sort makes for a very bad boss because they get drunk on power and believe they are more powerful and crucial to the organization than they truly are.

Chapter 14: Observing and Expressing Your Emotions

Lack of free emotional expression is exactly what forces people to wear masks while hiding all the things they are afraid of showing to the outside world. Repressed emotions have a habit of coming back with twice the intensity, so we often end up with the helpless, "*I don't know how to deal with my emotions!*"

Smothering and suppression of the emotions cause many, often very subtle, psychological biases and damage, which manifest themselves in our everyday life. Fortunately, there is an alternative where the emotions are just like clouds in the spring sky. They come and go, fully accepted.

What's the outcome? Some people deny their emotions so intensely; they have no idea at all what and how they're feeling in a given moment. They barely feel anything and are torn between thinking about the future and the past so much, they don't even bother asking themselves, "What emotions are present in me at this very moment?"

By suppressing emotion, we accumulate lots of excess energy inside our nervous systems, which is **very harmful** to our health, both mentally and physically.

A person who has minimal awareness of their emotional states can sometimes have a glimpse of *"I'm so angry!"* or *"I'm so nervous before tomorrow's exam!"*, but that is nothing more than a brief one-second look through the keyhole into the chamber in which a wealth of knowledge and precious information about the person is being kept.

Such a glimpse is not enough. We need awareness. Insight. Recognition. This will allow us to free all these emerging emotions while fully accepting their temporary presence.

Please remember the last time when you felt joy. How did it feel? The majority of people will just say, *"Pleasant,"* which will be the end of their retrospection. Such a shallow insight won't allow them to understand their emotions and fully recall this feeling.

Instead, it's good to focus on each emotion for a moment. Think about it. Why did you feel it? When did you start to feel joy? Where in your body is this feeling located? Analyze all these details very carefully.

Recently, I came across an interesting lecture by Eckhart Tolle, where he talks about observing our emotions. He says the expression of destructive emotions is not enough. Screaming with rage or crying like a baby gives a vent to the energy in you, but does not cure the root of the problem (of course, it is worth it to give this energy release, but it can be done in more constructive ways, such as going for a run). After you rest, the emotion may appear again. The energy, fed with destructive thinking, takes the form of destructive emotions.

Therefore, Eckhart suggests something more, "Express your emotions while watching this process." The second part of this quote is the key here, because expressing emotions alone may not give you the desired effect, as unobserved emotions will keep coming back. Observation gives you the awareness of how your thoughts generate emotions you then feel in your body.

Additionally, the process of observation results in so-called "depersonalization," which means that you will stop identifying yourself with the emotions. You cease to see them as an integral part of your existence, as a part of you, and begin to see them as clouds passing in the sky, separate from your self.

That's the exact difference between "I am angry!" and "I am experiencing anger."
I noticed the observation of my own emotions during their expression gives an incredible awareness of the processes, which previously I had no idea even existed.

You notice more, understand more, and hence, accept more.

Simply close your eyes for a moment and direct all your attention inwards.

Concentrate on the sensations that arise at the center of your being. **Observe in the silence.**

Allow your emotions to be, without losing your precious energy to sweep it under the rug. Even if they are not pleasant, accept their presence anyway. As a result, their visit to your body will be much shorter and less noticeable. **Just like every cloud, after a while, they will quietly drift away.**

Remember to watch your emotions without judgment. Put aside your beliefs about the feelings of anger, jealousy, stress, or fear. Instead, tell yourself you want to know the true nature of these emotional states. This is pure observation, which gives you the most valuable insight, not contaminated with your mental filters.

Note everything you have observed. The conclusions may turn out to be very important discoveries for you.

Chapter 15: Boost Your Social EQ with These Powerful Verbal and

Non-Verbal Clues

By tuning into other people's emotions or by empathizing with how they feel, there is a higher chance that you will respond appropriately to create the desired positive result. Thus, our ability to connect with our own and other people's emotions can be a powerful tool in social and leadership situations.

Understanding other people, helping overcome stress situations, motivating your team, negotiating business deals, and building a close-knit social circle becomes easier when you can use the personal information you have about them as leverage. It increases situational awareness and our ability to read people, thus helping us make the most positive decision.

Here are some verbal and non-verbal factors impacting social-emotional quotient, or our ability to read and deal with people:

Body Language

Research reveals that body language accounts for 50 percent of our communication. You'd wonder why there were words in the first place if body language accounts for half the communication process.

Tuning in to a person's body language will help you pick up important signals related to their emotional state and subconscious thoughts or feelings.

Here's a quick cue sheet to reading people's feelings through their body language:

•	Crossed arms and legs are signals of people creating a subconscious barrier. They are emotionally closed, suspicious, or do not subscribe to your ideas. They aren't open to listening to your views or are disinterested in the topic of conversation. You may have to emotionally open the person up a bit by changing the topic and then get back to the original topic. The physical act of uncrossing their arms and legs will make them more subconsciously receptive to your ideas.

•	How can you tell a genuine smile from a fake one? Simple, it's all in the eyes. Observe that there's crinkled skin near the person's eyes forming crow's feet. People often present a happy expression to hide their true feelings. However, if their smile doesn't cause the skin around their eyes and mouth to crease, they are most likely not as happy as they are pretending to be. Fake smiles create wrinkles only around the mouth, while genuine smiles create wrinkles around the sides of the eyes.

• When people constantly take their gaze away from you while speaking, they are most likely not being very honest or trying to hide something. Similarly, if a person speaks to you without taking their gaze away from you for long, they may be trying to threaten or intimidate you with their gaze. It is alright to look away periodically. However, shifting gaze constantly is a red flag.

• When you address a group of people, closely observe the ones who are nodding excessively or in a more exaggerated manner. These are the people who are most concerned about your approval. They are anxious about making a positive impression and want to be in your 'good books.'

• People who are nervous or anxious tend to fidget with their hands or objects. Other signs of nervousness include excessive blinking, tapping feet, and constantly running one's hand over the face.

• When an entire group walks into the room, how do you analyze who the leader or decision-maker is? Quickly observe everyone's posture. The leader will most likely walk with a straight posture, with shoulders pulled out. Subconsciously, they are trying to occupy maximum space to convey authority over their team. Standing straight and pulling back shoulders increases a person's physical frame. It makes them come across as much bigger than they are. This is why people in power love to keep this posture to show their influence over a group or place.

•	Expressions are the windows into a person's emotional state. When a person is amazed or surprised, their eyebrows are raised, and the upper eyelids widen. Similarly, the mouth gapes open. Expressions can often overlap, so watch for micro-expressions that can reveal precise emotions.

•	For instance, raised eyebrows can also reveal fear. Look for other micro expression clues to determine the exact emotion. If a person is experiencing fear, the eyebrows will be raised and pulled together with tensed lower eyelids, while the two corners of their lips will appear stretched. Similarly, a person's surprise is expressed by eyebrows pulled up and a lowered jaw. Learn to read the entire face, especially micro-expressions, to learn more about how a person is feeling.

•	Since micro-expressions occur in fractions of seconds, they are virtually impossible to fake. For instance, notice how, when people are deceptive, their mouths will slightly angle differently. Similarly, their eye movements become more rapid, the nostrils flare a little bit, and they pursue their lips together (a subconscious gesture signaling their lips are sealed, or they won't reveal the truth). Since the subconscious drives these split expressions, this makes them involuntary, and it is almost impossible to manipulate them.

• Enlarged pupils reveal intense emotions such as excitement, thrill, delight, surprise, and interest. When a person is attracted to you or truly delighted to see you, their pupils will involuntarily enlarge.

• The direction of a person's feet can also determine what's going on in their mind. Since feet aren't the first thing on anyone's mind, it's harder to manipulate body language related to legs and feet. If a person's feet are pointing away from you, they are subconsciously signaling their need to escape. However, if their feet are pointed towards you, they are interested or agree with what you are saying.

• Typical signs of frustration and stress are clenched jaws, wrinkled eyebrows, and tensed neck. The person's words notwithstanding, if you observe any of these signs, he or she may be undergoing a stressful situation that they are trying to conceal. The trick for reading people's emotions accurately is to keep an eye out for a clear mismatch between verbal and non-verbal clues.

• Observe a person's walk to tune in to their feelings. People with heavier gait and low gravity while moving their legs are most likely hurt, stressed, frustrated, or depressed. People who walk with a slower and more relaxed pace are reflecting upon something. Notice how confident, happy, and goal-oriented people walk swiftly in one direction.

- Observing a person's eye movements is a near accurate way of gauging how they feel since our eye movements are connected to precise brain functions. Our eye movements have an established pattern depending on the brain function or type of information we are trying to access. For example, when a person is caught in internal conflict or dilemma (to speak the truth or lie), they are more likely to look in the direction of their left collarbone. Darting sideways from one side to another can be a red flag that indicates deception.

- Proxemics is a subtopic within body language that talks about how people reveal their feelings and emotions through the physical distance they maintain with other people during the process of face-to-face interaction or communication. It is a very useful non-verbal signal for understanding a person's thought process or state of mind. Psychologists and body language experts believe that the amount of physical distance we maintain while interacting with a person helps establish the dynamics of our relationship with them or reveals our emotions about them.

A person who isn't standing very close to you may not be emotionally open or receptive. They may tend to closely guard their emotions or give only a little of themselves to the interaction. Such people may be more emotionally guarded and closed. You may need to make extra effort to get them to drop their guard and feel less intimidated.

It may be a defense mechanism against being emotionally hurt or vulnerable.

On the other hand, if a person is leaning in your direction, they may subconsciously convey being emotionally open, or they trust you with their feelings. They may also be more interested in what you are speaking about.

Tone

The tone, volume, pitch, and emphasis of a person's voice can help you decode the hints that can help you tell what they are feeling. For example, if you notice plenty of inconsistencies in the tone of their voice as they speak, they are probably very angry, hurt, excited, or nervous. Ever notice how your voice shakes when you speak in a rage or are nervous about something? It can also be a sign the person is lying.

Similarly, if a person speaks louder or softer than their regular volume, something may be amiss. Again, a person's tone is a dead giveaway. Sometimes people say something that sounds like a compliment. However, upon examining their tone closely, you realize the sarcasm and the condescension with which it was uttered.

The tone in which an individual ends their sentence says a lot about what they are trying to convey even with similar verbal clues. For example, if a person completes their sentence on a raised note, they doubt something or are asking a question. Similarly, if they finish the sentence with a flat tone, they pronounce a statement or judgment. Watch out for how people end their sentences to get a clue about their inner feelings.

Again, the words people emphasize can help you uncover their true feelings. For example, if a person says, "Have you borrowed the blazer?" while emphasizing 'borrowed,' it indicates their doubt over whether you have borrowed, stolen, or done something else to the blazer. However, if the emphasis is on 'you,' they aren't sure if it is you or someone else who has borrowed the blazer.

I also like to look at pauses between phrases to know about the person's attitude, emotions, and intentions. For example, if a person pauses after saying something, it could be because what they just said is extremely important to them, or they truly believe in it. Sometimes, a person pauses to seek validation or feedback from others. The speaker wants to gauge your reaction to what they said since it is important for them.

When people are in a more emotionally unstable or negative frame of mind (angry, hurt, or upset), their voice tends to be higher pitched or squeaky. They are most likely losing a grip on their emotions or cannot regulate their emotions effectively. When people are very angry, their voice becomes more screechy and squeaky, as if they are about to cry.

The Speed of a Speech

A person's emotions impact the speed of their speech. Notice how you start talking much faster than your normal rate of speech or words per minute when you are angry or upset. A rapid speech can convey a lack of organization, uncertainty, or lack of clarity. The person is not very comfortable speaking and is just trying to finish throwing his or her words. Again, a slower than usual pace translates into low self-confidence, inability to express emotions, inability to come to terms with one's emotions, lack of emotional reassurance, and other similar feelings.

Chapter 16: How to Control Negative Emotions

We are human beings, and therefore the emotional aspect of being human beings will always affect how we live. At any point in our lives, there are emotions that we have to deal with. We can choose to laugh or cry at whatever is happening in our lives. Unfortunately, negative emotions are the hardest to deal with. At times negative feelings overwhelm us to the point where we think of giving up. Learning how to control negative emotions will guarantee that we surround our lives with positivity. Despite the things that we cannot control, we should manage how we feel about them. Ultimately, this will have an impact on how we perceive our lives.

So, how do you control negative emotions from breaking you?

Eliminate Negative Thoughts

Managing negative emotions begins with negative eliminative thoughts. Negativity will always pull you down. You will always feel as though you woke up on the wrong side of your bed. Sadly, these feelings will also prevent you from seeing the good side of life. You will never see past obstacles that are stopping you from reaching your goals. Therefore, you must learn how to eliminate negative thoughts in your everyday life.

There are practical ways in which you could stop negative thoughts from affecting how you perceive things.

Talk to Your Negative Thoughts

The best way of dealing with your negative thoughts is not by avoiding them. Often, what you resist will persist. Therefore, you must become aware of these negative thoughts before anything else. How are you feeling? Are you tired, stressed, or frustrated? First, recognize your negative thoughts. To deal with them, embrace the idea of talking to these thoughts. This could be in the form of affirmations that remind you of the presence of negative thoughts, but you are choosing not to believe in them. Ideally, affirming that you are in control will bestow you with the mind control you need to see past your challenges.

Associate with Positive People

Additionally, getting rid of negative feelings requires that you associate yourself with like-minded people. If you are trying to transform your life, find someone already in the position you wish to be in. Make friends and maintain your friendship. Identifying yourself with people who have a direction in life will also give you a sense of direction. You will begin to see the positive side of living. Therefore, you will refrain from thinking negatively as most of your friends focus on the bright side.

With regard to emotional intelligence, find someone better than you. Learn from them how to live a happy life. Ultimately, you will quash negative thoughts in your mind.

Lower Your Expectations

Indeed, it is good to live a happy life. Nevertheless, this doesn't mean that you should have high expectations. Expecting things to be perfect will simply prevent you from being happy. Your vision of success should be closely tied to reality. Knowing that you will succeed in the long run will give you a reason to be patient for the best results. In turn, you will never rob yourself of true happiness that you should be enjoying now.

Create a Positive Morning Routine

Psychologists will argue that controlling your thinking will help you control your life. There is some truth to this. What you think about most is what you will eventually become. So, start your day on a high note by encouraging yourself. This eliminates negative feelings and boosts your energy throughout the day.

Overcome Stress and Anxiety

Negative emotions will often lead to feeling stressed out and anxious. To manage negative feelings from arising through stress and anxiety, the following tips should help you.

Exercise Regularly

Regular exercise will help you deal with stress in many ways. The idea of pushing your body to the limits through exercise can help boost your mental health. Research also shows that people who engage in physical activities frequently will lower their chances of feeling anxious. There are several reasons which could help in explaining this.

First, exercising lowers stress hormones in your body. Equally, regular exercise releases endorphins. These are chemicals responsible for enhancing your moods. Your sleep quality will also be improved by engaging in physical activities. The best part is that regular exercise will help you feel confident about yourself and your abilities. Inviting these good feelings to your life will aid in eliminating the negative vibe in your life.

Check Your Diet

Exercising routinely should be complemented by eating the right foods. The mere fact that you should overcome stress and anxiety implies that you ought to stay away from stress and anxiety triggers. Alcohol and caffeine, for example, are known to increase the likelihood of feeling anxious. Your caffeine intake should be avoided, as this will make you feel nervous or increase your irritability. It is important to note that stopping your caffeine intake immediately will have negative withdrawal symptoms. Therefore, it is recommended that you should reduce your intake gradually.

It Shall Pass

Sometimes it is good to remind yourself that you are not the only individual going through stress in your life. Some are going through harder situations. So, you need to brace yourself and keep your head up. Overcoming negative feelings that come with stress could be aided by having the mentality that the situation shall pass. The negative feeling that you are experiencing will pass. The important thing you need to bear in mind is that you are trying to make yourself stronger by believing that you can overcome the situation.

Overcome Social Anxiety and Shyness

Negative feelings can also be handled through the idea of overcoming social anxiety and shyness. The idea of being anxious when conversing with other people will invite negative feelings about yourself. You will never feel confident in approaching people and express yourself. People will think that you are shy. From your end, you will suffer as you will always hide in your cocoon with no friends to help you out. Below are strategies that will help you conquer social anxiety and shyness in your life.

Admit the Fear

The first thing that you need to do is to admit that there is fear within you. Accepting the fact that you have that fear is an extremely important first step in overcoming your problems. You cannot deal with something or a condition without identifying it. The importance of acknowledging the problem you are facing helps realize that you are better than what you think. It gives you a reason for seeing past your fears or shyness.

Engage Actively

Fighting your shyness by engaging actively is an approach that could also work. If there is someone you like, approach them, and be frank about it. Sure, you will be rejected a few times, but you will realize that there is nothing to fear. After all, no one will be harmed from your rejection. You cannot expect everyone around you to like you. So, anticipate that there will be a few rejections you will have to deal with. Adopting this mentality gives you the courage to overcome social anxiety. There is nothing to be afraid of, and that there is no harm in trying.

Get Out of Your Comfort Zone

Being shy will drive you to avoid people at all costs. Reserved people will prefer to be left alone in their worlds. However, you need to challenge yourself. Engage in activities regardless of whether they make you anxious. Participate in social games as this is what will gradually boost your confidence levels. Don't allow your fear to get the best of you. Challenge yourself by facing your fears head-on. It might be a daunting task from the word go, but eventually, you will rip the fruits.

Body Language

Your body language will also need transformation if you wish to overcome your anxiety. This will not come easily as you will have to practice regularly through the small conversations you enter into. When talking to people, try to make eye contact. Speak loudly for people to hear from you. If possible, give hugs and shake hands. Working on your body language will boost your confidence in great ways.

Dealing with negative emotions is not as challenging as you might have assumed. It all boils down to what you think about. As part of ensuring that you live a productive life, always ensure that you associate yourself with the right people. The influence you get from them will have a huge impact on your life. Similarly, you need to find a way out of stressful situations. Go to the gym and workout. Give your body an opportunity of releasing endorphins to help you feel good. Inviting positive vibes your way is an ideal way of banishing negative feelings.

Chapter 17: How Emotional Intelligence Can Make You More Productive

Emotional intelligence can be quite beneficial in making us more productive, purposeful, and provide us with a sense of direction. Being emotionally intelligent opens your mind to the abounding opportunities which you can tap into. Emotional intelligence improves the quality of life you lead and helps you create more productive interpersonal and professional relationships. Here are the benefits of emotional intelligence, which you should never miss out on; find out how emotional intelligence can make you more productive.

1. Mastering Emotional responses

Emotional intelligence makes you conscious of your emotions to control the responses you give to situations that trigger these emotions. When you master your emotions and emotional responses, you become less vulnerable to counterproductive reactions and unstable moods. Letting stress, anxiety, and anger control take hold of you makes it difficult to think rationally, and this can affect your productivity both at work and everywhere else. When you are emotionally intelligent, you become aware of possible emotional responses and place them under immediate control.

2. Promoting Self-care and stress/anxiety management

Every day, you are faced with one difficult situation or another, which requires you to make some really tough decisions. Sometimes, you have to overwork yourself just to achieve more and be productive. However, this can be quite counterproductive to do. Emotional intelligence trains you to recognize your limits and stay within the boundaries of these limits. Being emotionally intelligent means taking a more proactive approach to situations and also taking proactive breaks when necessary. This prevents you from overstressing yourself or having an emotional breakdown, which can quite affect your productivity. Emotional intelligence helps you get more done to avoid getting burned out or tapping out. An emotionally intelligent person knows working longer hours won't make them more productive, so they take a more proactive approach to productivity.

3. Improving Team Collaborations

Emotional intelligence improves your ability to collaborate with others and work in groups. Emotionally intelligent people are great at collaborating with others, and collaborative efforts are usually more productive. Emotional intelligence makes it easy to read, analyze, and process the emotions, strengths, and weaknesses of others, helping you devise better ways to achieve productive results. Since empathy is a core skill in emotional intelligence, you also find it easier to put yourself in place of others and determine how they might react to a situation. This makes for great adaptability skills, i.e., you find it easy to adapt to any environment you find yourself. It also means you find it easier to make logical and required sacrifices for the group, making your effort even more productive. Good communication, trust, and value always abound in a group where emotionally intelligent people are.

4. Improving Critique-handling ability

Whether harsh, negative, or positive, emotional intelligence helps you handle criticism better. The most emotionally intelligent people usually go out of their way to receive feedback and incorporate it to improve the quality of their work or personal relationships. As an emotionally intelligent person, you never stake criticism personally; instead, you make use of every critique to work harder and make an improvement on yourself. As an emotionally intelligent person, if someone says you are prone to anger, you don't explode in their face, thereby proving their point; rather, you accept their submission and then look inward to yourself, see if it's true, and make changes to improve. Emotional intelligence also teaches you to give your feedback to people, i.e., if someone does something to wrong you, you make them know immediately instead of keeping it in.

5. Increasing receptivity to change

No one knows change is necessary and required more than an emotionally intelligent individual. Since emotional intelligence enables self-awareness and promotes self-care, it gives you the required tools to initiate change and also deal with any change you find in your way. There is no point in facing change with a negative mindset, and this is exactly what you learn with emotional intelligence. Many people tend to welcome change with nasty attitudes and indifference; this makes it impossible for them to initiate or advocate for change even when it is necessary. Emotional intelligence gives you a positive outlook that helps you welcome change, whether desired or not. As someone who is emotionally intelligent, you will even encourage others to embrace positivity and inspire yourself to embrace it too. Change, whether personal or social, becomes much easier when you develop and improve your emotional intelligence skills.

6. Building and Maintaining Valuable Relationships

The relationship you have with others should be one that impacts the quality of life you live positively. There is no point in having relationships that add nothing to you, and this is something all emotionally intelligent people know. People should be in your life because they add value to you, and you reciprocate the gesture. Being emotionally intelligent helps you decipher people fast enough to know if they are the type you want in your life or not. However, it is not enough to simply build quality and valuable relationships; you must also strive to maintain the relationship you have built with others. Emotional intelligence provides you with the cognizance you need to maintain your valuable relationships and do away with the toxic ones.

As a person, it is possible to have low emotional intelligence, but with practice and consistency, you can develop your emotional intelligence skills. People with low emotional quotient tend to go through tougher challenges than people with high EQ since they have no idea how to manage their emotions or relationship with others. To live a life of direction, it is highly beneficial to learn and embrace every emotional intelligence skill.

Chapter 18: Developing Emotional Intelligence

Now you've seen how emotional intelligence creates an amazing quality of life in practice, let's get down to learning how to practice it!

Developing Self-Awareness

Emotions are very powerful things. Let me demonstrate how they have the power to control you.

In short, the way you perceive a situation is through the 'filter'; the filter is how your belief systems and thought processes interpret the situation. This then creates an appropriate emotion depending on how you perceive the situation, leading to your actions and reactions. If you do not develop consciousness before your emotions take hold of you, you are at risk of coming across as inconsiderate, disruptive, and conflictive to those around you, and more importantly, you can develop a sense of hopelessness in yourself due to the fact you can't control yourself. By becoming self-aware, you have to develop a sense of mindfulness. You have to live in the moment. To consciously pick up on your emotions as they happen. There are several ways to do this, which I will now explain.

The first thing to understand when seeking emotional awareness is that emotions are subjective. This means that the things that trigger different emotions in you are particular to YOU. There is no specific list of situations that could arouse different emotions. There are many reasons emotions are subjective, but it's mainly due to nurture rather than nature. How you were raised and what environments you are used to creating your emotional quota.

Journal Your Emotions

The first step is to recognize emotional patterns within you and what situations trigger them. It's easy for emotions to creep up on you subconsciously, and next thing you know, you're acting on them in a way that you shouldn't. So to recognize patterns to pick up on in the future, you should start by looking back at past situations that you know you could have avoided or acted differently if you stopped to think about it. Get a note pad and write down the situation, the emotion that you felt, how you felt it. You must regularly keep track of your emotions and outcomes through these methods every week.

A simple way to do it would be to sit down for one hour on a Sunday night and list all of the strong emotions you felt and the outcomes for that week. Reward yourself for positive situations and write down how you can turn the negative situations around in the future. Suppose you can do this every night, even better. Consistently being aware of your emotions after they happen will develop the habit of awareness in the present.

How to Improve Emotional Intelligence?

Developing Self-Awareness

It can help you know your strengths and weaknesses, and it is considered one of the main elements of emotional intelligence.

Self-awareness is nothing else than the process of knowing yourself, which is exactly what you need to focus on. That includes recognizing the emotions as they occur and feelings that come with them, and realizing what your thoughts and actions based on them are.

Knowing yourself also means knowing your strengths and weaknesses. This has to do a lot with confidence, but we will move towards confidence tips later. Your goal should be to be assertive or to explain that better, confidently communicate your ideas and thoughts and be able to justify them with good arguments.

Accept Who You Are

What it comes down to is that everyone is unique. However, you should become aware that that is an excellent thing. There is no need to worry about the things that you are not good at. Instead of that, a much better way is to accept who you are and look for ways to improve. For instance, you can always learn a new skill by applying to a class in your community.

Acknowledge Your Successes

One reason people have confidence issues is that they focus on things they are struggling with. Instead of that, try thinking of all the right things you have done in the last couple of days. Celebrate the little successes, such as managing to complete the task at work before the deadline. Don't accept the positive stuff as a routine. The point is that you are doing a bunch of great things, and you should know that.

Don't Compare Yourself to Others

This one is related to the first tip in this subsection. Never compare your life to someone else's because we all have unique life paths, and that's the beauty of it. Trust me; you can never win when you compare yourself to others. Instead, try this – compare yourself to the version of yourself from a couple of months or years ago. What changed? What other changes can you make?

List Things You Like About Yourself

When you have a bit of time with yourself, try listing a couple of good things you did during the day or simply the traits you like about yourself. It doesn't have to take long; two minutes is enough to think and acknowledge those things. It can be anything from "I am thinking to our dog because I feed him every morning" to "I am a funny person, and I can always make my friends laugh." Taking a couple of seconds to acknowledge those things will make you feel better and make you realize your worth.

How to Master Self-Regulation

Self-regulation allows you to control your thoughts, feelings, emotions, and behaviors in a manner that allows you to avoid reacting to things emotionally but to respond to them thoughtfully. This ability allows you to handle disruptive impulses and emotions effectively without letting them cloud your judgment.

If you're considering breaking up with your current boyfriend or girlfriend because you are sure the two of you do not complement each other, you think about this decision several times before taking the final step forward.

If you're considering a certain partnership offer, you do not accept the offer right away, but instead, you go over it a few times to make sure you employ the best response and make an informed decision that ends up being fruitful for both of you in the long run.

Here are different strategies you can employ to practice self-regulation.

Learn to Relax Yourself and Not React to Your Impulses

We react to our emotions and impulses because we allow the emotions, and the overwhelming feelings of those emotions, to override our ability to think lucidly. If you are scared of giving a presentation to a potential business investor, you are likely to allow the fear to increase your anxiety, which can keep you from giving an effective presentation.

This happens because extreme stress and anxiety activate your body's stress response. This response increases the production of cortisol, the stress hormone that produces different changes in your body, and that compels you to react to things. As you already know, reacting to things without emotional intelligence only makes problems worse.

To stay calm and sustain good relationships, learn to relax, so you do not pay heed to your impulses and instead choose its alternative, calmer route. Below are a few effective techniques you can use to teach yourself how to stay calm when in disruptive situations and then build a habit of staying calm at all times.

Learn to Be Mindful of Your Emotions

To be mindful of your emotions, teach yourself how to do everything mindfully. Whether you are cooking, eating, playing, mopping the floor, typing on your computer, or doing anything else, do it with utmost concentration and focus on every step of the task. This helps you do the task mindfully and stay aware of all the thoughts, feelings, and emotions you experience throughout that duration.

If you feel even a tinge of some sort of strong emotion bubbling inside you, pause and explore it so you can understand and then deal with it correctly. With time, you can master this exercise, and you will automatically start doing everything mindfully.

Allow Strong Emotions to Subside at Their Own Pace

When you hold on to different emotions and increase their intensity, reacting to situations without thinking becomes the norm. Remember, every emotion should enter your system, peak, subside, and then exit your body and mind without becoming extremely intense. Holding on to emotions is what aggravates and intensifies them. To keep that from happening, allow your emotions, particularly strong emotions that can make you react raucously, to subside at their own pace.

Every time you feel angry, sad, frustrated, anxious, or experience any other emotion that can intensify into an undesirable emotion you do not wish to feel, breathe consciously at your natural pace and bring your attention to your breath. Closely observing your breathing helps you stop focusing too intently on the emotion you are experiencing. As you pay attention to your breath, you will slowly feel the emotion's intensity decreasing at its own pace, allowing you to think clearly. As is the case with the other exercises in this guidebook, consistently practicing this one helps you master it.

<u>Think Things Through</u>

Whenever you experience an upsetting situation, one that seems too good to be true, or an overwhelming one and are tempted to quickly react to it, pause, and use this pause to think. For example, if your partner asks you to move in with her, do not whimsically say yes only to regret it later. Instead, let your partner know how touched you are by the gesture and are extremely tempted to move in with her, but I would like to discuss a few things with her before making the final decision.

It will take you a few occurrences to gain the ability to think things through, but with time and practice, you will get there. Once you start to think clearly on different matters before making the final call, others will do the same, and you are likely to experience less turbulence in your different personal and professional relationships.

Give Others the Benefit of The Doubt

Before jumping to a certain conclusion, train yourself to give others the benefit of the doubt. If your best friend acts agitated with you one day, do not assume that he hates you or does not want to be friends with you anymore. Instead, give him the benefit of the doubt and think about how he may be experiencing some real problems reflecting in his behavior.

Before making a certain decision, you need to encourage yourself to have thorough discussions with people you are upset with or those you think are upset with you. Always talk the matter out with the other person, so you mend the bond before it strains some more. You will be surprised at how effective this tactic is and how it helps bring people together.

Chapter 19: Why do we have Emotions?

Realizing the Roles of Emotions in Human Existence

Emotions, which are the expression of internal feelings, have established their dominance on the course of our existence over the years in various ways. Two kinds of emotions exist in human beings across all ages: Positive Emotions and Negative Emotions.

On one side of the coin, positive emotions are the pleasant and palatable emotions that we feel as humans, with examples of such emotions abounding in happiness, love, etc. While negative emotions are simply those unpalatable and unpleasant feelings, we feel as human beings from within. Examples of such emotions are anger, sadness, depression, and so many more. These are the types of emotions that abound.

Emotions are key players in the way we think and the way we behave likewise. Our thoughts and behaviors are greatly affected by the wave of our emotional tendencies as humans. Even our actions and decisions are also influenced greatly by the different waves of emotional flows we feel.

Components of Emotions

To have a proper grasp of all that we mean by emotions, it is expedient that we take a look into the components of emotions as we experience. We have three basic components of emotions in human beings, and they include:

- **The Subjective Component**

- **The Physiological Component**

- **The Expressive Component**

First off, we have the component known as the **Subjective Component**. This component of emotion deals with how we, as human beings, experience the flow of this emotion that we feel.

So also, we have another component, which is known as the **Physiological Component.** This component of the human emotions simply deals also in its part with the reaction that an emotional flow will spur in your body. The reaction of our bodies as human beings is what this component deals with.

Lastly, there is the component of human emotion that deals with the behaviors of human beings as a response to the emotions they feel from within. This component is what is known in humans as the **Expressive Component.** This component determines how we deal with the responses we reactively to the different kinds of feelings we feel.

These components are the different breakdowns that come together to contribute a great quota to the responses we give, both in the functions and reasons, to the different emotions that from within us as human beings. These components are highly important, and they are also very integral to every single emotional flow experienced by any human all across the universe.

What, then, are the Roles of Emotions in Human Beings?

The different emotional flows we have as humans do not necessarily stay for a long time in us, and we do not keep expressing most of them necessary for a long while also. It is humanly impossible for you as an individual to hold emotions for too long, which is why we can safely say that emotions can be very short-lived.

The real question at the end of it all is, why is it necessary to have emotions? What exactly are the roles of the different waves of emotional flows we experience as humans? Put differently, what are the needs for these emotional flows, and what are their functions to us as human beings as we go through our daily lives?

- Emotions are action motivators in every human being.

- They help us to thrive, survive as well as avoid dangers.

- Emotions are also key contributors to the decision-making process of every human being.

- Emotions promote the ability of every human being to understand people around him.

- Emotions also help people around you to understand you a lot more as an individual.

Emotions as Actions Motivators

Emotions, over time, have been one of the leading reasons for the actions a lot of people exhibit whenever they are around us, and even when they are not. Flaring up at a friend who has done something wrong to you can only be understood to be due to the emotion of anger or pain such a friend has caused in you. You felt the experience of this pain, disappointment or anger, and that is the reason for your flaring up at such a friend. That is one instance of your emotions being a motivator of your actions.

In another light, some of the actions we take as persons are just for us to avoid whatever unpalatable negative emotions might be coming up and instead, working towards getting a new wave of pleasant and positive emotions. Sometimes, as human beings, we decide to engage in some actions to catch fun or feel happy. We decide to carry out actions that will give us a sense of happiness, joy, and satisfaction we desire. And by doing these, you will also be taking a distance away from actions or activities that can result in being bored, sad, depressed, or probably anxious.

These ways are representatives of the impacts of our various emotional tendencies on us as human beings as they are a leading drive in us for whatever action we choose to perform.

Emotions are Drives Towards our Strive and Thrive as Well as Avoiding Dangers

Your emotions also help you to foresee and forestall danger. It is the emotion that helps you confront whatever has spurred a feeling of danger and makes you run away in the sight of fear or any impending threat that you suspect. This same emotion will give you the drive to seek a show of love whenever you sense the absence of such.

In all, according to Charles Darwin, the role of emoticons can be seen as being adaptive that in turn translates into actions in us as humans and will also help us increase our chances of survival through life and our chance at being successful individuals.

Emotions as Key Contributors in Every Individual's Decision-Making Process

Whenever you embark on the walk down the lane of the decision-making, more often than not, there is a compelling factor that lies in your emotions. This factor makes you see the need to take certain steps, say certain 'yes,' and say certain 'NOs.' You will decide to study hard for your exam when your emotions introduce to you that feeling of anxiety and fear of failing such exams. You get apprehensive, and so see the reason for you to stop every other thing at that moment and start studying squarely for the exams. The decision you took to study well for the exam is only possible due to the part your emotions played by presenting to you that feeling of fear and anxiety, therefore spurring you to decide to pick up your books and read immediately. Such is the kind of impact your emotions can have on you when you get to that point where you are to certain male decisions.

Emotions Serve as A Guide Towards Having a Good Understanding of Those around You

An understanding of your friends, family, colleagues, and others in your social circle is necessary to have a good life and how they feel from time to time. You will need to know when those around you are in the right mood for a joke. You cannot do certain things when it is not the right time to do them. You should also be able to understand the different emotional reactions of those around you and know what these different emotional reactions indicate about their personality. This, in turn, helps you to gather enough information about these people that will also help you understand them better.

Emotions will only be the best platform upon which you can build a proper understanding of those around you, judging based on their emotional reactions over time. If, for example, a friend has freaked out due to fear in the past upon seeing a cat, it gives information about her, and this can, therefore, be developed to relay a better impression of the person in question. The concept of emotions is highly influential in building an all-round understanding of those around you.

Emotions Also Serve as A Guide for Others around You to Build an All-Round Understanding of Who You are

If you have flared up seriously sometime in the past when faced with a question on your integrity, that reveals an impression to others around you that you are a person with firm regard for your name, and, by this, they would understand that part of you and treat it justly. No one will ever deny that their emotional reactions and displays have been a resultant effect of their tendencies as a person. Therefore, your emotional reactions and expressions can always serve as a point of reference for other persons around you to understand your kind of person and your emotional tendencies. This is another role of emotions in our existence as humans. Your emotional reactions and displays will have a ripple effect on how well people understand your personality.

Effects of Negative Emotional Spills on Our Existence as Human Beings

Understand that emotions are highly influential due to the roles they perform in our lives as humans. It is clear beyond all doubts now that without emotions, a lot of lapses will abound. More so, our lives will greatly be influenced negatively if we do not pay close attention to the effects of our emotions on our different lives. We will not be able to place good boundaries on the resultant effects of our emotional displays and reactions. We will also not be able to seek damage control measures to curb the adverse effects of our emotions, especially our negative emotions also. Some of the possible effects of adverse emotions on human life include:

Broken Relationships

If you have not taken adequate cognizance of your emotions as well as the frequency of your emotional outbursts, you will most likely live mostly as a loner as most of the romantic relationships you enter into will most likely end up abruptly. This will happen as you must have chased everyone around you away due to your uncontrolled emotions (negative emotions). Negative emotions have been responsible for many marital problems, divorces, and breakups.

Job Loss

A high percentage of people who have lost their jobs over time have done so due to one mismanagement of emotion or the other. Flaring up at the wrong time, speaking to a superior employee rudely or maybe even your boss, getting sad and sluggish while at work due to previous events at home, and so many more. Watch out before your emotions wreak too much havoc on your career or businesses.

Chapter 20: Learn to Deal with Your Feelings

Recognizing and Managing Emotions

Not everyone pays attention to their feelings, which often has a lot to do with one's childhood. Growing up in a loving environment that is both physically and emotionally safe is very different from being raised in a family where children witness violence, deprivation, or substance abuse by one or both parents. All these memories and traumas affect one's state of mind, and children usually learn early that sometimes it's safer not to show how you feel, or to expect kindness.

However, even people with happy childhood memories can struggle to identify or express their emotions.

One of the main traits of emotionally intelligent people is that they are in touch with their feelings. This means they don't ignore them, figure out what triggers them, and learn how best to deal with them.

How do they achieve this?

As feelings are usually a result of your thoughts, attitude, or experience, if you can manage to control those, you can take charge of both your emotions and your reactions to situations that trigger them. For example, if you think about the exam you have to write in a couple of days, you may feel anxious. If you notice that your boyfriend drinks a lot, you may feel nervous or angry if that brings up memories of growing up with an alcoholic father. If you attend a funeral, you may feel sad if that brings back memories of the loved ones you've recently lost.

Feelings range from simple ones—such as joy, fear, or grief—to the more complex combinations of simple feelings and your thoughts and images. For example, you may feel sad if a friend tells you his dog was killed in a car accident, but secretly happy it wasn't your dog. Or you may love someone, but at the same time be worried because of their high blood pressure.

Emotionally intelligent people rarely feel lost, mentally exhausted, or confused because they accept and process their feelings as they occur, instead of bottling them up. Besides, it's not uncommon for people to care more about others than about themselves. For example, you may be sad or angry when your friend experiences a tragic event, but simultaneously ignore your fears—either because you feel it'll go away (it never does) or because you don't have time to do something about them (although you always find time for others), or because you subconsciously believe you're not worth the attention (because there are people with much more serious problems in need of help).

We all know feelings are contagious. This is why we, consciously or subconsciously, avoid the company of sad, depressed, or troubled people and instead seek the company of happy, successful, and positive individuals. Think about how drained you feel when you have to spend time with a friend or a relative who complains or moans all the time—it makes you feel mentally exhausted, but secretly happy you don't have to live with someone like that.

Suppressing feelings is not healthy, especially if this goes on for a long time. Holding on to sadness or disappointment can make you feel depressed or bitter. However, many people are brought up not to show their feelings, and some spend their entire lives never letting go of pain, anger, or resentment.

When you don't deal with your feelings, you can develop many psychosomatic symptoms, such as a headache, ulcer, or high blood pressure. Bottled up emotions can cause muscle tension in the neck, back, or jaw.

According to the mind/body philosophy, when you suffer from tight muscles, you usually hold bottled-up feelings in that part of your body. For example, fear tends to affect stomach muscles, and problems can manifest in the shoulder and upper back pain, hopelessness in tight neck muscles, etc. If this is happening to you, and you don't want to seek professional help, you can try muscle relaxation techniques or learn how to work through your feelings before settling in your body.

How to express your feelings:

–   Talk about them

It's best to find an empathic person willing to listen, but if you have no one to talk to or if the issue is very delicate, you might consider seeing a therapist.

–   Write them down

If verbal communication is not your thing, write about your feelings. You can keep a journal if you like, or jot down specific emotions whenever you feel like getting something off your chest. If the things you write are very personal and you don't want anyone else to see it, flush them down the toilet after you've read what you've written.

–   Learn how to get rid of negative emotions

There are many ways to deal with anger, depression, or fear—you can try crying, going for a walk, calling a friend, listening to soothing music, analyzing your emotions to understand why you feel the way you do, withdrawing from people or situations that trigger such negative emotions, deep breathing, or meditation. If none of this helps and the feeling is overwhelming (especially in the case of long-held anger), you may try pounding on or screaming into a pillow, or getting some exercise.

The bottom line is not to ignore your feelings but take them seriously—especially if they persist. Developing emotional intelligence can help you understand and process your emotions in a mindful way, thus preventing serious health-related problems.

Managing Emotions in the Workplace

The modern workplace has changed a lot over the last fifty years. It usually consists of open-plan offices, high staff turnover, multinational and international employees and employers, high competitiveness, and layoffs. Such an environment requires staff to cope with constant change, cultural diversity, high-stress levels, and job insecurity.

For this reason, employers increasingly look for candidates with high emotional intelligence and the ability to work under pressure. In an increasingly stressful and challenging world, only those who can handle their emotions and manage stress are likely to thrive.

According to Bond University professor of management Cynthia Fisher, the most common negative emotions experienced in the workplace are:

– **Frustration**

This is when you feel trapped but can't do anything about it. Frustration in the workplace is the most common cause of burnout.

– **Worry**

With so many layoffs, it's natural to be worried about losing your job. However, instead of feeling anxious, try to focus on your job and think about ways of improving your performance to you make yourself more employable. Nervous people usually have low self-confidence.

– **Anger**

This is a very destructive feeling, which many people have a problem dealing with. Very few organizations will tolerate employees who can't control their temper. If you know you have an aggressive nature, watch for early signs of anger before creating a problem for yourself. To control your outbursts, try working out what your most common triggers are and avoid such situations if you can. You can also try attending an anger management course or developing emotional intelligence skills.

– **Dislike**

You don't have to like someone to work well with them. In big teams, there are likely to be many people with clashing temperaments or work styles. No matter what your personal feelings are toward someone, always treat your colleagues with respect and assertiveness.

– Disappointment

Repeated disappointments always negatively affect efficiency and productivity, and if unaddressed, can lead to burnout and high staff turnover.

The key thing about nurturing negative emotions in the workplace—be it feelings about your colleagues, management, working environment, salary, or something else—is that these feelings are contagious. This kind of resentment easily spreads and demoralizes others. This is why a negative person is more likely to be fired, if for no other reason than to prevent their negativity and resentment from spreading to others.

Besides, there are often people who will happily invest huge amounts of time and energy in spiting or sabotaging their colleagues.

As Reham Khan, a Pakistani film producer, said, "It amazes me to this day to think about women in the workplace who spend more time trying to damage other women's images or opportunities than they do on improving their abilities."

Chapter 21: Practical Ways to Use Emotional Intelligence

Now, we will dive further into practicality and how it applies to emotional intelligence. So how do you use your emotional intelligence to boost your life practically?

Self-management and relationship management serve great importance here. Stop, pause for a moment, and assess your situation. Examine where you are in your life, and what you plan to do next. If you are in a committed relationship, think about how your actions can affect your partner. Carefully consider what you do or say to gauge where the relationship goes accurately.

This also applies to the workplace. You are at work and have a project due by the end of the day. You are tirelessly working on that project, but more rush projects show up on the docket. This upsets you, only because it seems not to end, and you have a lot on your shoulders. You grow weary and tired, wondering if your efforts are even being appreciated. You resent your employers. This is where you have to put your emotional intelligence to good use.

Pause for a moment and take a deep breath. Getting upset about your current situation will not help you in the least. It might make your performance worse. Remember, you want to make good decisions logically, especially in the workplace. In this setting, take a moment to look at the number of projects you have on your docket. Take them down one at a time. We are all human beings, so we have to go at the pace we are used to. Because of this, we have to know our limits. It is not the end of the world if you cannot get to every project in time. Ask for help if you need it. We all need help, and sometimes we resist the urge to ask for it. Doing this will also improve your relationships with people. When asked for help, many people would jump at the chance to assist someone. It is human nature to want to help your fellow humans. But one thing we have not gone over yet is how we use emotional intelligence to test our health.

Ever visit the doctor? It is not fun. You are constantly worrying about what might be wrong with you, and you do not want to know. It is terrifying, and it can be costly. That is the number one reason people avoid the doctor's office. But your health is important. People with strong emotional intelligence realize this, but do not always act on it. As exemplified before, empaths care more about helping others, and it can often come at the detriment of their well-being. Because of this, establishing communication is important in matters of health. People often like to hide their health woes from close family and friends for fear of gaining too much sympathy. They do not want things to change and do not want to risk upsetting the status quo. This can be dangerous, especially if a close relative could be of some comfort to you.

Instead, resist the urge to act like this. Your emotional intelligence should tell you that others are capable of empathy, and you need not hide the horrors of your life to maintain order. Trust is important in any relationship, and you need to establish trust not just in the good times but the bad times as well. You do not just have to trust yourself, but others. People who do not trust others lead a cycle of behavior that is unhealthy. For example, imagine you suffered a tragedy at a young age. You are eight years old, and your parents have both passed away. The only person left in your life is your uncle, who has agreed to take care of you. But there is still a huge void in your life. Your parents passed away, and you have to find a way, at a young age, to move on. You can still establish healthy emotional intelligence despite the circumstances. A person could rise to the challenge and overcome any obstacles that life put in their way. An unhealthy pattern would be if you were to stop trusting the world after this tragedy occurred. Do not close yourself off from the world, and allow yourself to lose faith in everyone and everything. Instead, learn to allow other people into your inner circle. Give people a chance to make an impression on you and form that trust you lost a long time ago. We can build emotional intelligence over a lifespan, with never-ending opportunities for growth.

Communicating and Dealing With Your Feelings

So how do we communicate and deal with our feelings? It is a never-ending battle with the feelings we feel every day. We could wake up feeling amazing and wanting to conquer the world one day. The next day, we could feel miserable and not want to get out of bed. For most people, there is no consistency in our feelings and what will happen next. This is normal, and part of what being a human being is all about. You must be ready to accept this and realize that not every day will be perfect. There will be days when you feel terrible and feel utter sadness. The sadness and desolation can feel like the worst feelings in the world. They can consume you if you let them, and you must be careful to avoid going down that dark path. Try not to overthink everything and keep it simple.

One thing we have not talked about is feeling suppression. There is a delicate balance here. You do not want to overstep someone and be aggressive. You do not want to suppress how you are feeling all the time. If you do that, eventually, you will burst and probably go off on a rampage. Both situations are unhealthy and not productive. You need to find a balance. Find a balance that fits both angles and try to understand that will be beneficial to everyone. Your feelings are just as important as others. Just because you are sensitive to others, it does not mean you have to ignore your desires. If you do this, you will never be happy. Happiness is always the goal, and to achieve that, you need to maintain and keep improving upon your emotional intelligence. It needs to be a repetitive thing that never stops. There needs to be a constant effort on your part to keep picking yourself up and never letting up.

This is where you have to stop and think about the bigger picture. Think about how the emotions you feel are impacting your life and decide whether it is worth letting them do so.

Let me explain. You are driving in traffic. The people in front of you are driving terribly. They are driving like the worst drivers on earth. They are slow and indecisive. These drivers cut you off and are going 20 miles below the speed limit. You wonder how can people drive this badly, and how can they get a license? You do not realize it, but your emotions are rising. Your anger is getting bigger and bigger, and eventually, it will consume you. You are letting people you don't even know ruin your day.

Stop and think about this for a moment. You are getting upset because you may be in a rush. Or you may not be in a rush and simply want to get to where you are going. These drivers are a hindrance to you, and it is ruining your peace of mind. Consider whether this is worth it. Figure out why these drivers are upsetting you and process it from there. Take a moment to figure out if getting upset about this is the best course of action. It does not solve your current problem. The drivers will still drive badly, and there is nothing you can do about it.

Sure, you can always yell at the other drivers. There is that option. However, there may be consequences to doing that. The other drivers may think you are nuts and call the cops on you. Or, you may find a nuts driver and it can endanger your life. All of this is over traffic. You let your anger get the best of you, and it could hurt you. Take a moment and consider if it is worth it. Is it worth it? Would you let people you don't even know upset you that easily? It is just a drive. Everyone has somewhere to go, and people all drive at their speed. It is best to go out and just take this in without letting it upset you.

You can do this by understanding your emotional triggers. What upsets you? Do you know what upsets you easily? It may not be easy to determine. We all get angry at different things. Anger is a normal human reaction. We are not advocating suppressing all your anger. If you do this, you will burst. We are merely advocating finding measures to limit your anger and control how it affects you and others. There are many forms of emotional triggers that we have. It is all different for everyone. For example, some people get emotionally triggered when someone breaks off a relationship with them. It can come as a shock to the system. Someone you adored no longer can stand the sight of you. They do not want to be around you as much as you want to be around them. It hurts; it hurts. It is a feeling that you cannot control. You feel a mix of anger and sadness. This is because often, it is unexpected, and you did not see it coming. Because you did not expect this, it stings you a little deeper.

But what if you were never with them, to begin with? It is hurtful to get rejected by someone you have an interest in. You have built this ideal and worked the courage to approach this person with interest, only for them to tell you they have no interest. They are not into you and have communicated that there is no chance for you. This applies to not getting that job you wanted, too. A human resources manager rejects you for a job you had hopes of getting. Because of this, it reflects upon your self-confidence. You take a hit, wondering where it all went wrong.

You can also get emotionally triggered because of helplessness. This can be because of a situation outside your power and control. Because it is outside your control, it frustrates you, causing you to get upset at the situation. You dislike not having control. It triggers you, and you want to make a change. But you soon learn that you cannot. It is too late, and you are powerless.

Chapter 22: Why is Emotional Intelligence so Vital to Ensure Success?

The ideas of Emotional Intelligence are not new, with examining returning to the first piece of the twentieth century. The expression "Emotional Intelligence" was presented by Salovey and Mayer in 1990. Be that as it may, it was Daniel Goleman, a Harvard-trained clinician and author who truly carried EQ into the standard. He expounded on EQ in The New York Times and his 1995 book Emotional Intelligence. Be that as it may, it was his 1998 article in Harvard Business Review that started incredible enthusiasm for the business network.

The basic reason for Emotional Intelligence is that EQ abilities identify with how viably individuals work with others, explicitly around:

• Self-Awareness

• Self-Management

• Social Awareness

• Relationship Management

1.   Self-Awareness

Self-Awareness implies having a reasonable comprehension of one's emotions, qualities, shortcomings, drives, and capacities. Superficially nothing is surprising about this idea - it's been touted for a huge number of years. In any case, it's a basic aptitude, and numerous individuals ignore it. It's so significant because individuals with a high level of self-awareness perceive how their emotions and qualities influence them, and this identifies with how they interface with others. They will, in general, be exceptionally keen as in they set aside some effort to consider the things that are essential to them, and how their work and lives identify with these things. This self-reflection encourages them to know about both their confinements and qualities, and they're real to life about this.

2.   Self-Management

Goleman says that Self-Management liberates us from being detainees to our emotions. Without understanding what we're feeling, we can't control our emotions, which leaves us helpless before our emotions. This is alright regarding positive emotions like excitement or achievement; however, it's an issue if negative emotions like anxiety or frustration constrain us.

Individuals with this authority are normally enthusiastic and optimistic. And eager. This is especially significant in the working environment since emotions are infectious

3.   Social Awareness

The third segment of Goleman's EQ model, Social Awareness, is, for the most part, about empathy. It's the capacity to peruse someone else's facial expression, verbal and non-verbal signs of comprehending that individual's emotions. This is particularly significant for leaders because by staying receptive to how people feel, they can say and do what is generally proper. For instance, they can attempt to quiet individuals' feelings of trepidation, decrease outrage, or in a progressively positive model, make some great memories at the office party.

4.   Relationship Management

Relationship Management is where these three aptitudes all meet up. This is the most prominent part of an individual, and specifically pioneers or leaders. This is where you see abilities like peace promotion, group building, and influencing others. Leaders with great aptitudes in the first three areas of EQ will be more successful at managing relationships since they're sensitive to their own emotions. This implies they'll approach relationships from a place of credibility. It's not just friendly, yet it's what Goleman calls "friendliness with a reason": motivating individuals toward the path you want. These individuals are truly good at creating networks, not really because they're exceptionally amiable, but rather because they comprehend that nothing gets done alone. They're talented at having the option to work with others. These EQ skills are one of a kind from an individual's specialized abilities and intellectual capacities. As indicated by Goleman's exploration: 90 percent of the distinction between star entertainers and normal entertainers was inferable from EQ capabilities. This and other research show that EQ skills are directly connected to basic business measures and individual achievement, more so than conventional estimates, for example, IQ. It isn't so much that IQ and conventional elements are not significant. They are. In any case, IQ and different employment-specific skills are entry prerequisites, especially in managerial and leadership positions.

One inquiry that frequently comes up is whether individuals are brought into the world with high EQ, or whether it very well may be learned. We, as a whole, know people who appear to be normally talented in how well they work with others. They naturally see how to comfort individuals and, if they are leaders, propel their kin and keep them effectively occupied with their work. A few people will be more naturally talented than others. However, fortunately, EQ skills can be learned. There's been some detailed research on this, and a great proof that individuals can figure out how to associate more adequately at work. But with the end goal for this to happen, individuals must be personally motivated, and they have to rehearse what they realize back at work and get support for their new aptitudes. The vast majority of us can consider individuals who appear to have a characteristic capacity to cooperate with other people. So while EQ might be a significant ability, is it something that can be developed, or is it something an individual is brought into the world with?

Dr. Fabio Sala of The Hay Group found that workshop mediations are viable at improving EQ. An examination at Case Western University found that EQ preparation improves execution, yet such gains are held numerous years. So the uplifting news for business is that while there might be a hereditary pre-attitude towards Emotional Intelligence, these abilities can be developed, and they will, in general, be held as long as possible. There is absolutely a requirement for training and support to construct these skills. Lastly, EQ skills won't be improved without an earnest want to do as such.

Leadership and EQ

One criticism of Emotional Intelligence that we regularly hear is that it sounds great in principle; however, it's hard to try. Furthermore, some proponents of EQ don't appear to do an excellent activity of inspecting what it looks like in the everyday working environment, or how it tends to be enhanced and practiced.

One of the main problems here is that Emotional Intelligence will, in general, be, to some degree, nonexclusive in its core interest. It assumes that all individuals can show these aptitudes in pretty much similar manners. Goleman and his associates are evident that not every single powerful leader has all EQ skills and that a significant part of the estimation of EQ is situational - certain circumstances will require some EQ abilities more than others.

What is regularly neglected, however, is that there's another component of conduct that impacts how individuals act and how they translate the conduct of others.

EQ and Versatility

In the present economy, businesses and organizations are searching for approaches to improve their efficiency. Emotional Intelligence has risen as an asset to improve the exhibition of people and their organizations. What's more, as research keeps on archiving, EQ is making a difference. There are objective, quantifiable advantages related to EQ, including expanded deals, better enrolling and maintenance, and increasingly powerful leadership. Further, there is proof that EQ abilities can be developed through training programs. Versatility training shows explicit abilities that increase Emotional Intelligence. Building up this mastery makes people and their associations progressively effective and productive.

Lastly...

1.   An insurance agency found the normal approach sold by one team of specialists is $54K, while another team sold strategies with an average of $114K.

2.   The U.S. Aviation based armed forces expanded its capacity to effectively predict recruiter achievement by three-fold and diminished enlisting cost by $3 million.

3.   An investigation (of more than 500 official inquiry candidates) recognized emotional skill as a significantly preferable predictor of placement accomplishment over intelligence or related knowledge.

Discoveries were predictable in all cultures and countries.

Emotional Intelligence was the variable in every one of these models.

As of late, enthusiasm for Emotional Intelligence (EQ) has developed as research has shown its effect on an assortment of business measures. These incorporate enlisting, and employment determination deals results and leadership performance.

Chapter 23: Emotional Intelligence and Self-Esteem

Emotional intelligence (EQ) is tied in with being aware of your emotions. If you have high emotional intelligence, you recognize what you are feeling from minute to minute, and much of the time, you likewise know why you feel as you do. Besides, you recognize what you have to do to change your emotions in circumstances when you wish to feel unexpectedly. Emotional intelligence in this manner makes you increasingly mindful of your own needs, and it expands your capacity to take great consideration of yourself.

High emotional intelligence can't be unaccompanied by high self-awareness. Therefore, if you have a high EQ, you additionally realize yourself well. It is simpler to build high self-esteem (for example, build up a decent relationship with yourself) when you know yourself. How can you acknowledge and love somebody you do not know? Consequently, self-esteem and emotional intelligence go inseparably. As you raise your emotional intelligence, you likewise figure out how to comprehend yourself better, acknowledge yourself (including both positive and negative emotions), and fulfill your own needs and worth yourself more. Everything gets simpler when you improve your relationship with yourself.

Emotional intelligence isn't just about getting oneself but also about comprehending others. With a high EQ, you can go into a room brimming with individuals and promptly get a feeling of how the individuals in that room are feeling right then and there. You can comprehend others' needs better, making it simpler for you to assist them with satisfying those necessities. This makes it simpler to deal with every single diverse sort of individuals since you realize how to make them feel good. We, as a whole, have a social need, and as we raise our emotional intelligence, we become better at building and keeping relationships that assist us with fulfilling that need. We make ourselves feel much improved, and we raise our confidence by helping other people feel better.

To raise your emotional intelligence, you essentially need to hear yourself out more frequently. Enjoy a reprieve and ask your body what it is feeling. Do you feel some strain or agony anywhere? Listen to your instinct (your premonition). When you open up to the information that is now inside you, you will discover that you "know" considerably more than you knew about previously. Try not to disregard or attempt to push emotions away. They have something essential to let you know. Your emotions will assist you in raising your self-esteem.

Emotional Intelligence - A Conscious Solution

By improving the Emotional Intelligence (EI) of its workers, an association can effectively use two key patterns recognized in Patricia Aburdene's Megatrends 2010: "The Wave of Conscious Solutions" and Spirituality in Business." Emotional Intelligence, a cognizant answer for automatic reactionary emotional propensities, is the capacity to obtain and apply information from your emotions and the emotions of others. The data about what you're feeling encourages you to settle on successful choices about what to state or do (or not state or do).

It empowers you to utilize your emotions to assist you with settling on better decisions in-the-minute and have progressively viable control over yourself and your effect on others. The idea of Emotional Intelligence depends on brain research showing that these aptitudes are not the same as specialized and subjective capacities since they include an alternate piece of the brain - the emotional focus, the limbic framework, instead of the neocortex. Emotional Intelligence is comprised of 5 fundamental capabilities. The first is comprehending what you're feeling. The second is dealing with your emotions, particularly upsetting feelings. The third is self-inspiration, the fourth is compassion, and the fifth is managing relationships.

Emotional Intelligence abilities have been demonstrated to be basic to individual and hierarchical achievement. Research on Emotional Intelligence has uncovered that the impacts are significant, affecting many business/individuals issues, including expanded creativity and development, expanded profitability, improved basic leadership, and increased benefits. The business case for creating emotional intelligence turns out to be clear when we perceive that the emotions leaders, workers, and clients feel sway basic leadership, mental lucidity, and the reality of organizations and the adequacy of government and non-profit organizations.

The emotions that leaders experience impact the culture and climate of an association overall. All the more explicitly, leaders' emotions influence what workers feel, how fulfilled they are, how loyal and faithful they are, and how beneficial and productive they are. Like this, how representatives feel and play out their work influences how clients feel, how satisfied they are with both products and services, and at last, how loyal a client is to the organization or association. What's more, how steadfast clients directly affect the primary concern and benefit of an association/organization. Notice that the fundamental component of the relationship is of leadership.

Leadership is not simply the CEO or Executive Vice President or Director. The in-control individual in each workgroup, each director, and each person in the organization is a leader. Self-leadership is one of the most significant components we center on in skill advancement. Self-leadership is simply the inside capacity to prompt settle on the best decisions and choices minute-to-minute for the day, regardless of whether at work or home.

Negative Impact on Business

Examining the effect of unmanaged emotional reaction and the absence of emotional intelligence aptitudes reveals the important, negative effect on business. Unmanaged emotional reactions or absence of emotional intelligence abilities by administrators and workers at all levels can prompt

- lack of creativity and development

- unsuccessful reengineering and procedure improvement initiatives

- slow development of the high potential ability

- decreased productivity and efficiency

- workplace violence

- high turnover

- career derailment

- decreased customer satisfaction and customer loyalty

- stalled change initiatives

- declines in income

- increases in healthcare costs and stress

- negative organizational climate/culture

Developing Emotional Intelligence Skills

The uplifting news is Emotional Intelligence aptitudes can be scholarly. Be that as it may, there is a proviso: when we apply the common preparing approach focused on upgrading investigative or specialized abilities, we are bound to come up short. Traditional projects exclude the components by which the limbic system (the emotional focal point of the mind) adapts best: extended practice, motivation, and feedback. Creating emotional intelligence aptitudes necessitates that people wipe out old practices and grasp new ones. What's more, this requires practice and self-reflection on the effect of utilizing the new aptitudes.

Chapter 24: Different Types of Emotions: Negative and Positive

Emotions can usually be categorized into two different types. However, these types come in different forms. Some experts categorize emotions into two types: emotions to be expressed and emotions to be controlled. Others categorize emotions as primary emotions and secondary emotions. One thing common with both classifications of emotions. However, is all kinds of emotions are usually either positive or negative? Whether the emotion is primary/secondary or expressed/controlled, it will either be negative or positive. Often, people believe that positive psychology is centered mainly on positive emotions, but this isn't quite true. Positive psychology leans more towards negative emotions because it is more about managing and overturning negative emotions to achieve positive results.

Firstly, positive emotions may be defined as emotions that provides pleasurable experience; they delight you and do not impact your body unhealthily. Positive emotions, as expected, promote positive self-development. We are saying that positive emotions result from pleasant responses to stimuli in the environment or within ourselves. On the other hand, negative emotions refer to those emotions we do not find particularly pleasant, pleasurable, or delightful to experience. Negative emotions are usually the result of unpleasant responses to stimuli, and they cause us to express a negative effect on a person or a situation.

Naturally, we have different examples of emotional groups under positive and negative. But most times, you can't authoritatively state if the emotion is positive or negative. Certain emotions could be both positive and negative. The best way to discern between a positive and negative emotion is to use your intuition. For instance, anger could be both positive and negative. So, the best way to know when it is negative or positive is to discern the cause and the context of the anger intuitively. This book is, of course, going to focus more on negative emotions and how you can embrace them to create positive results for yourself.

Anger and fear are the two prominent negative emotions which most of us erroneously assume we have to do away with. To be realistic, we cannot allow these emotions to rule our lives yet. We must also understand that they are a necessary part of our experiences as humans. It is impossible to say that you never want to get angry anymore; what is possible is to say that you want to control your anger and get angry less. Mastering negative emotions such as anger is about recognizing and embracing the reality of them, determining their source, and becoming aware of their signs always to know when to expect them and how to control them. For example, if you master an emotion like anger, you naturally start to discern which situation may get you angry and how you could avoid this situation.

A list of negative emotions include;

- Anger
- Fear
- Anxiety
- Depression
- Sadness
- Grief
- Regret
- Worry
- Guilt
- Pride
- Envy
- Frustration
- Shame
- Denial…and more.

Many people regard negative emotions as signs of low emotional intelligence or weakness, but this isn't right. Negative emotions have a lot of benefits as long as we do not allow them to overrun us. You aren't completely healthy if you do not let out some negative emotions now and then. One thing you should know is that negative emotions help you consider positive emotions from a counterpoint. If you do not experience negative emotions at all, how then would positive emotions make you feel good?

Another thing is that negative emotions are key to our evolution and survival as humans. They direct us to act in ways that are beneficial to our growth, development, and survival as humans. Anger, mostly considered a negative emotion, helps us ascertain and find solutions to problems. Fear teaches us to seek protection from danger; sadness teaches us to find and embrace love and company. It goes on and on like this with every negative emotion there is.

When we talk about negative emotions, we don't mean negative as in "bad." The negativity we talk about concerning certain emotions isn't to portray them as being bad but rather to understand that they lean more towards a negative reality as opposed to positive emotions.

Negative emotions, without doubt, can affect our mental and physical state adversely; some primary negative emotions like sadness could result in depression or worry. We must understand that they are designed just to make uncomfortable. They could lead to chronic stress when not checked, making us want to escape these emotions. What you should, however, know is that we cannot completely escape negative emotions; we can only master them, so they don't affect us adversely. Often, some of these emotions are geared towards sending us important messages. For example, anxiety may be a telling sign that there is something that needs to be changed, and fear may be a sign that a person or situation may endanger our safety.

Overall, what you should know is that these negative emotions you experience aren't something to be gotten rid of. Rather, they are meant to be mastered so we can employ them in achieving the high-functioning, full-of-purpose life that we desire and deserve. Just like positive emotions, negative emotions are meant to protect us and serve as motivation for us to live a better, more qualitative life and build/maintain quality relationships with people around us.

Note: Negative emotions in themselves do not directly have any impact on our mental and physical health and well-being. How we process and react when we experience negative emotions is what matters to our health.

Chapter 25: Busting the Myths About Emotional Intelligence

As is the case with a lot of things, there exist several misconceptions regarding emotional intelligence. Throughout this book, you've probably been able to identify the misconceptions you have had about emotional intelligence yourself, and the accompanying truth of the matter. This chapter is dedicated to busting the many myths that many people have when it comes to EQ. Some of the myths are laughable, while others are downright ridiculous. Seeing that EQ deals with emotion, it is probably not too unexpected that there would be numerous feelings expressed. Dive in to find out what is true about emotional intelligence and what isn't.

Myth: Emotional intelligence is a woman's area
Truth: Emotional intelligence is a skill that applies to both men and women.

For the longest time, the stereotype of women being more emotional than men has been perpetuated by various channels. It, therefore, follows that when most people hear of emotional intelligence, they only think of women. This could not be further from the truth.

First of all, the claim that women are the more emotional of the human species is not a claim supported by biology. When scientists set out to study this phenomenon, they found out that the populations observed were more likely to behave according to the expectations placed on them by their cultures rather than as dictated by nature. In other words, women might behave more emotionally since that is what society or culture dictates from them, while men might repress their emotions for the same reason.

Seeing that we are capable of emotion, regardless of gender, there is a need to understand and manage those emotions. Even if there were a parallel universe where males were virtually incapable of having emotions, they would still be required to deal with women who have emotions. Emotional intelligence is a scale that these parallel universe males would require when interacting with the parallel universe women.

Myth: Emotional intelligence is the sole determinant of success in life.

Truth: Many factors determine whether you will be successful in life and EQ happens to be one of them.

Emotional intelligence opens a lot of doors for you in life. When you can read and relate well with people, you do not have as many obstacles than someone who has low EQ. However, EQ is not the all-inclusive package for success. Success requires a combination of smarts, hard work, opportunity or chance, and sometimes even sheer luck. Being low in the EQ does not automatically qualify you for failure. There are some professions where people become highly successful just by relying on their IQ.

An engineer, for instance, might be required to have a very high IQ so that they can easily grasp concepts. The same engineer might be very low on the EQ front and still become highly successful because their work calls for smarts over emotional intelligence. Sure, the engineer might struggle with personal relationships and will probably never hold a management position, but they will still be successful in their own right.

Myth: Emotional intelligence is about being nice.
Truth: Emotional intelligence is more than just being nice.

Over the years, nice has grown to be synonymous with being a pushover or a doormat. Whenever people hear that someone is nice, they start to imagine all manner of ways they can walk all over that person. Here's the thing: If you think of nice as the capacity to tolerate people's personalities and their quirks, then yes, emotional intelligence is about being nice. However, if your definition of nice is the person that says yes to every request and does not have a voice of their own, then you are way off from what emotional intelligence is. Emotional intelligence does not make you a yes-man. Emotional intelligence equips you with all the skills that you need to be able to say no as many times as you need and to do so unapologetically.

Myth: You're either born with emotional intelligence or not.
Truth: You can learn to become more emotionally intelligent.

Emotional intelligence is not the same as height whereby you are either born tall or short and are, after that, doomed to never reaching the higher shelves or always being the brunt of height jokes. Sure, some people have a higher ability to grasp emotional intelligence. This might depend on how they are born, how they are raised, the experiences they have been through, and numerous other factors that they interact with as they become adults. However, most people are capable of being emotionally intelligent. Even psychopaths who are incapable of feeling emotions like the rest of us know how to mimic emotional intelligence. If you are a fully functional human being with a wide range of emotions, then you are fully capable of being emotionally intelligent.

Myth: Everyone that knows how to charm people is emotionally intelligent.

Truth: Sometimes, there is more than emotional intelligence behind the charm.

Some of the most charming people you know are also the most dangerous human beings you'll ever cross paths with. Just because a person knows when and how to smile in your face does not mean that they are high in EQ. They might just be manipulative. Psychopaths, for instance, know how to blend in and play Mr. Sociable Guy's role to perfection. While an emotionally intelligent person will make you feel relaxed and comfortable without invading your personal space, a psychopath trying to win your trust may be more forceful, persistent, and full-on in a manner that might be uncomfortable. A trick you can use to determine whether you are dealing with high EQ or psychopathy is by trusting your gut feeling, watching whether someone's actions match their words, and noticing how you feel after every interaction. If you leave conversations feeling drained and unsure, you might be dealing with an energy vampire in the form of a psychopath rather than an emotionally intelligent person.

Myth: Introverts are not usually emotionally intelligent.
Truth: Introverts can be as emotionally intelligent as anyone else.

Introverts are known (or at least stereotyped) to be these shy and socially awkward people who have little to zero chance of being good at normal social interactions. While there may be some truth to it, this is not exactly the textbook definition of an introvert. An introvert is simply someone who prefers to look into themselves rather than turning to their external world for stimulation. An introvert is content in their own company and will often prefer to be silent rather than to talk. An introvert's worst nightmare is the extrovert, especially the kind of extrovert who does not have any emotional intelligence. Just because a person prefers to be silent does not mean that they are low in emotional intelligence. The fact that introverts are inward-looking means that they probably already have the self-awareness bit of EQ figured out. However, because introverts tend to be so absorbed in their worlds (in the most unselfish way possible), it means that they have to work a little harder at drawing themselves out into their external environment.

Seeing that introversion is a personality type, and personalities are not known scientifically to be dynamic, introverts will often face the uphill task of opening up their world to other people. For instance, you cannot be empathetic to the suffering of others unless you are aware of this suffering. To become aware of this suffering, you must at least speak with this person to tell you that yes, indeed, they are having a bad day. This can be almost too much to ask from an introvert.

The good news is that emotional intelligence can be learned since it is a skill like any other. An introvert can pick up the cues that they need to incorporate to be emotionally intelligent, just like all other personality types. There are introverts out there who are highly emotionally intelligent. They know how to carry themselves when they are in a group of people. They understand that certain circumstances call for them to leave the security of their shells. Once they are back home, they quietly retreat to the safety of their shell until different circumstances require them to come out.

Myth: Emotional intelligence is only important for people in leadership roles or particular professions.
Truth: Emotional intelligence makes your life easier regardless of who you are.

When you are in a leadership position, your lack of emotional intelligence will be more apparent and detrimental compared to a lack of emotional intelligence in the people that you lead or any other person. It has been said that with great power comes great responsibility, and this could not be truer when it comes to emotional intelligence. When you serve as a leader or boss, your every move is in the spotlight. People will pay attention to how you speak to your juniors, how you show care and consideration for others, how you manage stressful situations, and even how you manage yourself. Your teams will also look to you to model the kind of behavior that they should emulate and to be their mentor in matters of business and relationships. Imagine being in such a position while lacking emotional intelligence. More likely than not, you are going to be highly overwhelmed.

That being said, everyone needs emotional intelligence in their lives. You do not need to be anybody's boss to appreciate the benefits that come with being self-aware and self-regulating. And what about motivation? Everyone could use some bit of innate drive and passion in their lives. Motivation is what gives you the fuel to get you everything that you need in your life. If not for anything else, aim to be emotionally intelligent to have better personal relationships in your life. We could all use some of those.

Chapter 26: Tips, Tricks, and Skills to Improve Your Emotional Intelligence

<u>Emotional Intelligence Skills</u>

In this section, I will discuss a few emotional intelligence skills you'll want to begin mastering. These skills will benefit you long term in every area of your life. There's no downside by improving these skills. It will make you a better-rounded person capable of things you may have not previously thought possible.

1. ***Empathy*** - High EQ people are usually skilled at putting themselves in the shoes of those around them. This is an excellent skill to focus on, as the insight you'll gain from being more empathetic will allow you to connect with others and teach you things about yourself you hadn't yet learned.

2. ***Active Listening*** - By listening before reacting, you give yourself the space to take all your feelings and thoughts into account. Listening also helps to drain the tension out of certain situations by letting the talker get their feelings off their chest. If you're defensive and react without listening, you'll often only further the conflict.

3. *Mindful Breathing* - People experience their emotions physically. This means when we get stressed, our bodies will react as if we're being threatened or attacked. It's part of our very nature to do this. However, if we can calm our reaction to this stress, the body won't be taxed nearly as hard. One of the key ways to do this is by practicing mindful breathing. Whenever you start feeling tense, begin breathing in deeply and slowly, concentrating only on the breath, letting it flow in and out of your body. After a couple of minutes, you'll begin noticing a difference. This is because your body is now in a more relaxed state. Practicing this will allow you to keep your emotions under control and make more informed decisions.

4. *Apply Consequential Thinking* - For instance, when something gets you mad or upset, take a deep breath and then think through the action you're going to take, assessing any benefits and costs it may have. This will train you to be more careful when making choices in the future.

5. *Acknowledgment* - Acknowledging feelings that are both positive and negative will allow you to gain valuable information about yourself and make you more self-aware.

6. *Reading Body Language* - Practice reading the body language and facial expressions of people who have conversations. Look for how they physically react with each emotion. I read a book on body language and practiced studying it a few minutes each day when an opportunity presented itself. At first, I wasn't great at picking up the different cues, but over a few months, I got good at knowing how people felt just by how they were carrying themselves. It's a great skill to learn. I've found it to be invaluable in both personal and professional settings.

Emotional Intelligence Tips & Tricks

1. Be open to criticism and feedback. Be receptive to learning how other people view you and use that information to make any necessary adjustments.

2. Take the time to sponsor and mentor employees that have earned it.

3. Make an extra effort to be polite and thank people. When people are at ease, they will be willing to perform harder for you.

4. Identify how you feel at multiple times of the day. Make a mental note when something triggers a strong reaction from you. You can use this information to learn what things you need to work on.

5. Employees appreciate management who are willing to share their privileges and perks.

6. Be consistent with your behavior and how you treat others.

7. Show that you're a thoughtful person. People respond to this much more than you might think. It will make achieving your objectives and goals much easier.

8. I suggest practicing mindfulness in all facets of your everyday life. Being mindful of everything around you allows you to become extremely aware of your feelings and the feelings of others.

9. Take the time to celebrate any positive emotions. You'll find if you take the time to recognize your positive emotions, they'll begin to occur more frequently. This will allow you to have better personal and professional relationships.

10. Show that you care about people. This gesture is more powerful than you might think in enabling you to achieve your leadership goals and objectives.

11. Before you act. Take a moment to pause, acknowledge any feelings or thoughts, and then clear your mind.

12. Take one long deep breath before you respond to something or someone when you're emotionally fired up. This pause will allow you the time needed to gather yourself.

13. Try and be compassionate in everything you do. While you won't always be successful, coming at things from this angle will make you more in tune with the feelings of those around you.

14. If you hit some type of set back, take a moment to step back and analyze what you can and cannot control the situation. If you can't

control something, let go of it and move on. This will allow you to focus on the things you can control to move past the setback.

15. A good practice technique to use is when you have an issue take a moment to consider it and then write down two solutions to it. This will get your mind used to think about problems before instinctively reacting to them.

16. Take stock of your strengths and then try to use them more often to your advantage.

17. Take stock of your weaknesses and find a way to improve on them gradually.

18. Learn to sense your emotions in advance so you won't get surprised or overwhelmed by them.

19. Once you've learned to acknowledge your different emotions stop to ask yourself what can be done about them and come up with solutions.

20. Try and stop your low EQ habits. These include judging other people critically. This is a difficult one for most people. Another one is taking offense when people are critical of you. It's easy to get defensive but it's not beneficial. You should be learning how to rid yourself of the bad habits replacing them with habits that will benefit you mentally and spiritually.

21. When at work, have a feelings board available for your employees. This can be a whiteboard simply split into three parts of the days with a list of emotions. Have your employees mark how they

felt during each part of the day and then assess how your staff felt and when they felt certain things. You can begin to observe patterns by creating solutions to help ease any negative low points that may arise for a majority of the staff during certain parts of the day.

22. Remember, your emotions aren't just feelings. Try and understand what the message is behind your emotions. This will allow you a greater understanding of yourself.

23. Create an environment of positivity around you. Start cutting out the influences that are negatively influencing you and replace them with ones that benefit you. Having a positive environment will allow you to open up and grow as a person.

24. Model your behavior after other high EQ people. No need to blaze a new trail when a perfectly good one has already been created to show you the way.

25. Embrace new ideas, people, and experiences. These will all teach you and offer opportunities for positive growth. Use them to your benefit.

26. Look for the best in others, and don't ever be ashamed to ask for help. People with high levels of emotional intelligence realize their limitations and are open to support and help from the people around them.

27. Don't fear change. It's a natural part of life. Emotionally intelligent people accept that the world will throw a curveball from time to time. Having the ability to adapt means you can roll with the

punches and look at change as a new opportunity instead of something to be upset about.

28. Don't withhold intimacy from your loved ones. The more emotionally intelligent you are, the more open you are to sharing your self with those around you. Don't hold back out of fear. Instead, let the people you care about know the real you.

29. Be intellectually curious. Growth is life. Always be exploring and learning new things about the world and the people around you. If you don't seek out the knowledge you'll never be able to evolve as a person.

30. Put yourself in other people's shoes. Your viewpoint isn't the only one or even always the right one. Allow yourself a few moments to look at things from a new perspective. Doing so will allow you to come into any discussion with an open mind free of judgment.

31. Take responsibility for your actions and feelings. If you do or feel something you not proud of, own up to it and try to do better next time. No one is perfect, everyone will stumble and fall along the way. Don't get down on yourself, instead, look at it as an opportunity to learn something new about yourself.

32. Don't hold things in. Doing this isn't healthy and will cause you to lose control of your emotions and blow up eventually. Work through your issues as they come up.

33. Don't let other people dictate how you feel about yourself. You need to be confident in yourself and your abilities. Don't let other people's opinions determine your self-worth.

34. Practice conveying what you're thinking in a non-threatening manner. Be respectful of those around you.

35. Emotionally intelligent people aren't afraid to share the way they feel. Practice sharing whenever possible.

36. Check your ego. Be open to other people's viewpoints and opinions. Don't let your ego get in the way of connecting with others.

37. Don't give guilt trips to the people around you if you have an issue deal with it head-on. Don't dance around the problem. Be direct but not rude or inconsiderate. Let the people in your life know where they stand with you. Don't do things like slamming the door or give an attitude.

38. Emotionally intelligent people don't believe in manipulating others or resorting to mind games. Don't prey on the weakness or kindness of others. Treat people like you'd expect them to treat you.

39. You don't need to win your conversation or argument. It's not a competition. Be open to hearing their side and consider what they have to say. Don't invalidate what they're telling you because you aren't in agreement with them.

40. Don't hold your intellect over the people around you. If you're smarter or more informed on an issue, don't lord the fact over those

around you. Instead, be humble and if someone wants more information, share it with them without being condescending.

41. High EQ people are normally very well balanced individuals. They don't tend to be too optimistic or too pessimistic. Work on finding ways to keep an even keel even when faced with stressful or unpleasant situations.

Chapter 27: Self-Perception & Emotional Intelligence

Learning to understand yourself is a key component of emotional intelligence. Having a healthy perception of yourself will allow you to confidently move towards building strong relationships, managing stress, and achieving the goals you set for yourself personally and professionally. Self-perception is the prism with which you view yourself in. Most people don't take the time to understand themselves as well as they should. When they experience emotional outbursts, they don't reflect on what was causing them to feel that particular set of emotions and how they impact other areas of their life. In this section, I will discuss the importance of self-perception and how to discover who we are and how to get to who we want to be.

If you're not able to be self-aware, you'll never be able to be aware of those around you. Learning to become more self-aware is the first step in raising your emotional intelligence. To get started, I suggest documenting how you feel daily. Take notes a few times each day on how you're feeling and examine what happened to make you feel that way. By recording this, you'll be able to go back over your notes and start to see what types of patterns have developed. This will allow you to understand the types of people or situations that trigger certain emotions in you. Having this information will allow you to examine yourself more closely and figure out ways to manage your emotions better and hone them to benefit you instead of holding you back.

Self-perception is often broken down into three smaller categories. Once you've learned how to get the most out of each of these areas in your life, you'll be well on your way to a happier, more stable life. I'm going to discuss each of these sections below briefly.

1. **Self-Regard** - You need to put yourself first. However, you need to do this without being arrogant or insecure. You need to understand your strengths and put them to use in ways that will benefit you. If you don't respect yourself, you'll have a hard time respecting other people. I suggest getting some honest feedback from people you trust who care about you and know you. The goal is to take action based on what you learned about yourself.

2. **Self-Awareness** - When you have self-awareness, you're able to manage how your emotions will impact those around you, and you're also able to read other people's emotional nonverbal cues. The more aware you are, the better you'll be able to have and keep meaningful

relationships in your life. As a practice, try reading the facial expressions of the people you come in contact with daily. These cues are things like frowning, smiling, pursed lips, and furrowed brows. You'll also want to observe people's body language when they're in an emotional situation and see how they respond physically and verbally. It's easiest to do this when you're not an active participant in the emotional exchange. After the situation is, overthink over the scene in your head and imagine how you could handle it better if it were you. Doing this exercise is good practice for when you do get in an emotional confrontation with someone.

3. *Self-Actualization* - This component has to do with becoming more purpose-driven. This can be for something in your personal life or professional life. Seeking meaning in what you're doing and how you want to live takes some courage. It requires you to step up and make the commitments necessary to gain what you desire. A good way to further develop this muscle is by leveraging your skills, strengths, and talent. Take some time to figure out what those are for you and then go about finding ways to use those things to improve your life and get the things you want out of it.

One of the best ways to train our minds in the art of self-perception is mindfulness. What is that, you ask? Well, mindfulness is the art of training your mind to be aware at every given moment. Being mindful allows you to step back from a situation and figure out how you feel before responding. It allows you to see what is happening around you because you're paying attention to yourself and the world. Mindfulness is all about experiencing life instead of just watching it happen around you.

Chapter 28: Releasing Destructive Emotions and Strengthening

Positive Ones

Feelings and emotions are a huge part of an individual's personality and interaction with other humans. If you don't control or manage them, they control and manage you. Negative emotions, at times, overpower us and take complete control of our life. However, you can learn to deal with these negative emotions by diverting your attention and investing the energy into something more positive and constructive. Train your brain to move out of the negative thinking cycle and get into a more positive frame of mind. Here are a few proven tips to release destructive emotions:

Intense Physical Activity

Releasing negative emotions from the mind is facilitated when you perform a physically demanding task such as exercising, kickboxing, running, working out at the gym, swimming, and other similar activities. When you get active and exercise, the body releases feel-good hormones and chemicals that help elevate your mood. The feel-good endorphins promote a positive state of mind and act as a channel for venting out negative emotions.

Exercise is great for the body, mind, and spirit! Participate in activities that preoccupy your body and mind, which means you'll have little time to process negative emotions. Sometimes, walking outdoors for even 15 minutes can give you a huge emotional boost. The idea is to occupy your mind with something else by changing its focus or putting yourself in a different environment.

Often, when something negative or unfortunate happens, we experience a strong wave of emotions. Wait for this wave to subside and then calmly contemplate how you wish to behave. Instead of bottling up or repressing your feelings and emotions, you need to decide how you want to express them. Avoid taking the escapist route in such a scenario by consuming excessive alcohol, doing drugs, or spending hours watching television.

Instead, get up and get an outlet for these feelings by practicing a rigorous physical activity or talking to a trusted friend or family member.

Put on Your Creative Hat

Another wonderful way to release negative emotion is to channel it through artistic pursuits or passions. You can use art or other forms of creativity for restructuring your negative feelings and emotions into something constructive and positive, thus taking the focus away from these destructive feelings.

The negative emotions that occupy your mind disappear temporarily and give you time to contemplate or think through your actions. You get enough time to reflect upon your feelings and respond to them in a rational manner that's well thought out. Creativity can be anything from making a sculpture to developing a short story to going out and painting a happy scene on canvas. Divert your feelings towards writing a poem or song. If nothing else works, just turn on the music and dance. I swear, it works like magic.

Art and creativity allow you to transform destructive feelings into a more positive and constructive purpose, curbing anxiety, depression, frustration, and stress. You will identify a clear purpose, even in pain. If you are not the artistic type, even a regular adult coloring book and some crayons can do the trick. It's not a high skill activity and can be extremely cathartic all the same. Art and creativity have plenty of stress beating benefits.

Practice a 'Let Go' Ritual

It is extremely therapeutic sometimes to give in and vent your negative feelings or emotions (towards yourself or others) through a specific symbolic ritual. This is a tangible way or physical way to release negative emotional experiences. There are several rituals for releasing negative emotions.

I know some people who write a letter to themselves or another person expressing their thoughts, hurt, frustration, anger, and anguish. Once they are done pouring their heart out into the paper, they burn or tear the letter, thus signifying that they are over their emotions or they have released those toxic emotions.

Throw the ashes in the air or flush them in the toilet. It is cleansing your body and mind from all negative emotions or flushing out destructive emotions. Mention all the emotions you've experienced and all steps you've wanted to take.

Spend Time with Loved Ones

One of the best ways to get negative emotions out of your mind is to spend time with loved ones who motivate and inspire you. Understanding, encouraging, and supportive family members and friends can quickly change your mood and help you deal with painful emotions.

Though negative emotions are a part of life and allow us to grow stronger, we don't have to deal with it alone. We can reach out to others and seek their support. This is also a great way to build a comforting circle that you can trust and turn to in challenging times. You can seek comfort, guidance, and positivity from people who care about your well-being. So, the next time you are feeling discouraged and down, simply talk to a trusted friend or family member and pour your heart out and watch as the frequency of your thoughts magically transform.

Talking to another person may help you gain a different perspective on your situation. You may begin to see things in a manner you hadn't considered earlier. Sometimes it is important to get a different and fresher perspective on your issues to resolve them. Look at others for guidance, advice, consolation, and feedback. It isn't necessary to pretend to be strong all the time and handle everything on your own. Reaching out to others is not a sign of weakness. Rather, it shows you are strong enough to ask for help to reduce your pain.

Avoid Dwelling on Problems

However badly you may feel about your problems or are upset about something, avoid dwelling on the issue. Ruminating about the problems only worsens it. Just try to understand it more objectively. Don't make mountains out of molehills by focusing on negative emotions. I have a few tips up my sleeve when it comes to avoiding rumination and obsessing about issues.

One thing I love to do when I find myself being tempted to ruminate about an issue is, schedule a worry period for a few minutes each. I know it sounds incredulous to some. How can you set aside a worry period? It isn't some kind of rehearsal, is it? However, it can work miraculously well! Try to think about the issue for no longer than 25-30 minutes each day. As time passes, the feelings will gradually become fainter and less overpowering. Push the feelings away if they persist and remind yourself to wait until tomorrow's worry period.

Try to recognize the triggers that lead to rumination. For instance, why did you feel bad about the feedback your boss offered? Why does it so consume you? Is it related to worry about your performance, and subsequently, money? Are you worried about the impression your boss has about you? Identify the worst that can happen in the given scenario and determine different ways to handle the issue. Having a plan of action ready for dealing with the worst will put you in a more confident state of mind about petty issues.

Problem-Resolution Approach

Sometimes we feel something about an issue or person because of an underlying cause. For instance, you may feel pangs of jealousy every time a co-worker outperforms you or is praised by your manager. This may have an underlying issue, such as being burdened by expectations since childhood or that you were never praised enough by your family on your accomplishments. These feelings from your childhood that left you with low self-esteem and a sense of inadequacy may lead you to feel jealous or envious of other people. The underlying causes are low self-esteem or low morale.

Once you identify the underlying cause, it is easier to take remedial action against this overpowering feeling, causing your negative emotions. You may decide to talk to a counselor or therapist to eliminate the underlying feeling of inadequacy and develop greater self-confidence, thus leading to the gradual elimination of feelings related to jealousy at work and personal relationships.

Let us look at another example. You may not be good at a particular technical skill, which makes you experience feelings of inadequacy or frustration. What can you do to eliminate the underlying issue that is causing the emotion? Get a tutor for the skill or ask a friend who is an expert to train you in it. You can also practice by taking on extra work, read or use online or offline study resources.

This is a remedial action for tackling the problem from its roots to discard the negative emotions it creates. Think of every possible solution and chalk out a plan for tackling the emotion from its roots rather than obsessing about it.

Challenge Negative Thoughts

Each time you find yourself slipping into a negative and irrational thought process, challenge the extreme or catastrophic thinking. Consider how you are responding to the situation. Try to avoid thinking in extremes and challenge unfounded thoughts. Why do you think XYZ doesn't care about you? What is the evidence that makes you think so? What is the evidence that challenges this thinking? Think about all the things that XYZ has done that shows they care. Sometimes, we don't have solid evidence and tend to overthink or exaggerate situations. Ask yourself questions such as, "Do I have evidence that my thoughts are true?" "Do I have evidence that these thoughts are untrue?" "Is there a different perspective on this issue?" "Am I intermingling facts with my opinion or beliefs?" "What can I do to deal with the situation in a more mature manner?" "How would someone I greatly admire or look up to react in a similar situation?" Each time you find yourself being overcome by negative thoughts, replace it with more rational or realistic thoughts. Alter your self-talk from negative to neutral or positive. Keep repeating positive affirmations in your head like a tape. Make a conscious, mindful effort to think of a more realistic and optimistic way to look at the situation.

For instance, if a potential client who has taken your business card tells you that they'll call you for business in a few days and they don't, don't automatically assume that you've lost them or they won't call. Maybe they are pre-occupied with something important and will call you in a few days. Maybe they have postponed the project for later and will call you when it is time to begin. Stay hopeful and relational.

Don't automatically assume the worst until you have clear evidence of it.

When you change your self-talk, you alter your mood. Positive self-talk can completely transform the way you feel. Whenever you find the negative self-talk rambling in your head such as, "I am not good at something," or, "Someone is avoiding me," replace it with, "I am getting better at this each day," or, "They are preoccupied with something really important."

If you have been thinking negatively for long, you won't be able to switch to positive thoughts easily. In such a scenario, you'll find greater success with neutral or realistic thoughts.

Chapter 29: NLP and Thought Reframing

Submodalities are nothing but distractions that are made in our representative system. It assists in neurologically remembering sensory experiences, both real and imagined. For example, there are higher chances of you remembering a vibrant, large image than a tiny dull-colored one. Submodalities are solid building blocks that feed our brain with what is important and what is not. Think of them as barcodes that help us identify specific sensory experiences and determine their importance.

If you understand coding, you'll know that even a slight change in the code can change the design or meaning. Changing or altering meaning leads to a change in our state of mind. A change in the state of mind leads to changes in responses, which eventually reflects our behavior. Doing things differently can help us change our reality and our perception of the world or reality.

What is Reframing in NLP (Neuro-Linguistic Programming)?

In NLP, content reframe refers to offering a different meaning to a thought or statement by obtaining more content that completely changes or reframes the focus of your thought.

In reframing, you take an undesirable behavior or characteristic and lend it a more positive intention. You give more alternatives to fulfill the positive intent, trained by negotiations and rationalization for resolving mental conflict. Reframing thoughts can also change the entire meaning or context of the issue.

Even with NLP, reframing is all about changing the meaning or frequency of thought, either purposefully or unknowingly. Framing offers focus or border to your thought. You see a situation or issue within a specific reference, which directly results from your perceptions and beliefs. When you challenge these frames or limits, you change how you perceive or react to a situation or experience.

For instance, your thoughts will drastically function differently when you are told that a task needs to be completed within an hour than when you are told that you have a fortnight to complete it. The objective of reframing is to assist a person in perceiving or experiencing the situation in a different way, which impacts your choices. Reframing your thoughts makes you more resourceful when it comes to reacting to a situation.

In NLP content reframing, a statement or situation is recovered using more information to change the entire context or focus (termed as reframing). Reframing simply means taking an undesirable action or trait and lending it a more positive intention.

Behavioral Techniques for Reframing Thoughts

Cognitive Behavior Therapy is utilized by professional therapists or counselors to help clients overcome negative or destructive thought patterns and replace them with more constructive and positive thoughts. Reframed thoughts can help enhance your outlook, which can lead to a more positive approach and action. Our negative thoughts or perceptions are often deeply rooted in childhood or adolescent experiences. CBT can form new neural pathways to change your thoughts and increase the horizons of your thought process. If anything, you are reprogramming your mind to influence your actions more positively.

Brainstorming

Brainstorming is a great way to identify your thoughts and then subsequently reframe them. Writing a journal can help your thoughts flow freely or unhindered. Attempt to identify your problem in a single sentence. Think of every possible solution that you can. Allow your imaginative problem-solving skills to come up with different possibilities freely.

For instance, if your lack of monetary resources is a burning issue, you can apply for a job, get a degree, consider applying for a loan or look at taking up another part-time job to supplement your current income. Getting back to the point, there are several possibilities when it comes to resolving an issue. You just have to consider these possibilities and award yourself some much-needed hope.

Use the Power of Visualization

Every time you arise each morning, and even before you move out of your bed, start visualizing your day. How do you want the day to unfold? What is the most positive outcome that you expect out of it? If you have a dentist's appointment scheduled for the day, imagine him or her telling you that you have a healthy set of teeth. If you have a meeting scheduled with your mortgage application, imagine it being accepted.

Think of how you will enter your workplace, welcomed by a smiling boss and group of co-workers. Replace things that happened negatively with a more positive outcome. In your mind's eye, twist the negative occurrences into positive. Think that things went well.

Just before you go to bed, try to practice visualization. When we sleep, our conscious mind is at rest, but our subconscious mind is super active. By practicing visualization just before we go to bed, we train our subconscious to be occupied by events as we want them to be. The subconscious mind does not distinguish between imagined reality and reality.

For our subconscious forces, everything that enters it is real. When the subconscious mind believes something to be real, it drives our actions in sync with these thoughts and leads to our imagined thoughts. This is how we bring about a change in our thought frequency from negative to positive via visualization. You are simply filling your mind with limitless positive energy, which gives you hope and fills the mind with positivity to give you plenty of possibilities.

Reframe Disappointment

Don't think of disappointment as a catastrophe, after which your world comes crashing down. There is life beyond disappointment, so think of it as a normal occurrence. Don't be too hard on yourself. You can't possibly do everything exceptionally well. It is alright to have a few downs, too, along with the ups. Some folks find it increasingly challenging to move past their failures and get caught in a vicious web of negative thoughts and action. Allow yourself to experience disappointment and look at any situation in an objective manner.

Learn to segregate situations that are within and beyond your control. For instance, you performed a project to the best of your abilities and the client's brief. However, they changed their brief and want to make changes in the project before accepting it. It is natural to be disappointed and affected by this since you worked so hard on it. However, this isn't something that is a consequence of your action. Sometimes, you have to let go of matters that are not within your realm of control. Focus instead on things that can be controlled. For instance, better communication and brainstorming with the client during the initial stages of the project to help them understand exactly what they want. Think of different ways to improve client brief and communication, so clarity is established right at the onset of the project.

This will help you move towards a more constructive frame of mind and break away from the negative thinking pattern.

NLP and Context Reframing

The core of NLP is programming your mind by reframing thoughts using the main NLP presumption that every action or piece of behavior is valuable in a specific situation. By thinking of NLP in terms of every action or behavior being used in a specific situation, you change the response to that specific behavior. Consider multiple factors that can be reframed to obtain a drastically different response.

For instance, if you share a situation with a friend and think about things from their perspective, you will get a different spin on the same issue. Notice how a positive spin is given to ideas in a political scenario using NLP. When you believe every behavior has a more positive intention, the shift changes from negative to neutral thoughts. For instance, you think about hurting someone with your words or actions. There is still a positive intention behind it. It is to feel secure, powerful and completely in control. It can also be to prevent the other person from doing something wrong or to make them a better person through punishment.

Every situation is good in some way. Our brains process everything in evolutionary terms with an underlying purpose. A majority of the time, we work for the overall benefit or survival of everyone involved. However, there are times when we act with a short-haul personal interest, but there is always a clear objective of our responses and actions. Identify the underlying positive in every situation, response or behavior.

Dissociation

A knee-jerk, or quick, reaction to any seemingly negative situation when one is frustrated or stressed is natural. Think about your reaction when your boss yells at you, you argue with your spouse or have to wait endlessly for a client who has made a habit of showing up late for every meeting. NLP helps mitigate the effects of these negative feelings by restoring greater objectivity and neutrality in any situation.

Recognize the emotion that you want to eliminate. Imagine yourself living the entire situation from a third-person point of view. Let this mental scenario unfold before you in rewind and then set it to fast forward. Add humorous background music to it to make the situation lighter. Play it in your mind a couple of times. Try to visualize the scene as it's currently playing. The negative feelings should evaporate or decrease. It can also be changed. The pattern can be repeated multiple times for a higher impact.

Anchor Yourself

Anchor yourself to associate a specific positive emotion or response with a particular sensation. When you identify a positive emotion by linking it to a deliberate gesture, the anchor can be stimulated each time you feel low. You will gradually notice your feelings or emotions beginning to transform.

Recognize what you want to experience by recalling a time you were extremely happy, or your life was full of joy. Make that visual sharp, powerful and intense. Remember that time by performing a physical action such as rubbing your palms or touching your nose. Repeat this until you find an anchoring phrase signifying happy times closely linked with the physical gesture. Once your mind is conditioned to associate the gesture with an anchor phrase, you will find yourself thinking about the happy time simply by performing the gesture.

By performing the gesture, your mood will alter from frustration, stress and anger to a state of calmness, confidence and joy. This is an excellent strategy for altering your mood quickly.

Establish Rapport

There are plenty of ways to get along with people for rapport building. One of them is focusing on the other person's breathing. Another great way to establish rapport on a subconscious level is to mirror the person's body language, including gestures, posture, expressions and words. This works on a very subconscious and primordial level. The theory is deeply rooted in evolutionary science. When you mirror someone's actions, at a subconscious level, you are revealing to them that you are similar. However, this should be subtle. Don't give the other person the impression that you are imitating them, or else they could be offended.

Chapter 30: Dealing with Your Past

If you are still living in painful memories or carry any emotional baggage from the past, you are not paving the way for an emotionally healthy and balanced future. You'll have a hard time creating a happy and positive life ahead of you if you are still wrestling with the past. When you accept the past rather than obsessing about it and deal with it, you are creating avenues for a more rewarding life.

Here are a few brilliant tips for dealing with the past and living a more positive, balanced and emotionally fulfilling life:

Acknowledge Past Challenges

Unresolved experiences of the past can create not only lasting physical damage but psychological consequences as well. Don't let these destructive emotions of shame, guilt, regret, revenge, etc. breed inside you for long. Learn to come to terms with these emotions not to let your present or future be affected by them.

Don't pretend that you are not affected by these events. You won't be in a position to get over it if you pretend that it didn't happen. Try to acknowledge and allow yourself to feel everything that you felt in the past (and still feel).

For instance, if you feel an overpowering emotion triggered by memories of the past, instead of curbing the feeling, step away for some time. Use this time to reflect on your emotions and how they impact you. Once you are done reflecting upon and feeling the emotions, get back to what you were doing. The consequence of past actions can be very powerful, especially if you are without a support system.

At times, the trauma from past actions is so overpowering that it impacts our relationships. Past trauma can also prevent you from fulfilling your goals. This affects not just your present perspective about life but also your ability to deal with challenges in life.

Understand that There's No Way to Change the Past

There is nothing you can do to change the past. As much as you wish to, you can't do anything to change events or people. The best way to manage a painful past is to tell yourself that it can't be changed now, accept it and change the way you perceive it.

Many things are outside our circle of control. However, the way we react to them is something that is still in our hands. We can either live in the past or ruin our present and future, or we can choose to learn from the past and move on. Even though plenty of circumstances are beyond our control, accepting these events as being a part of life is something that is completely within our realm of control.

The past cannot be revisited, but perception about it can be changed. If you don't stop obsessing over the past, the hurt will spill over and damage future experiences.

Direct your efforts towards accepting the past and offering forgiveness to the ones who have hurt you. You don't do this for them; you do it for your peace and well-being. You give forgiveness to let go of the past and move on. Feel the emotions you want to feel and then let go after a point.

Try to remind yourself that hanging on to these destructive emotions will only end up harming you. Acknowledge the negative emotions and seek compassion for others as well as yourself. Gather all the strength to forgive everyone who harmed you.

Don't expect this to be an overnight process. It will differ from person to person and may take time.

Spend Time with Different People

Spending time in the same setting with the same people where you experienced negative past emotions will only trigger more reactions. Instead, change your setting or spend time with a different group of people who are supportive, inspiring and positive. A powerful social support system can safeguard you from damaging experiences.

Support other people around you who are feeling low to derive strength from their situation and support them. Volunteering is one of the most wonderful ways to let go of a painful past and build a positive and constructive present, which will serve as a foundation for a good future. It will also be a great way to interact with a new set of people. When you see other people's vulnerabilities, you become more thankful for your blessings and learn to cope with your troubles.

Seek the Help of a Professional

If you feel overwhelmed by your past and nothing else seems to work, seek the help of a professional counselor or therapist. There are instances when experiences can be devastating and can threaten to change your entire life ahead. In such cases, professional intervention is required. Talk to therapists who will help you with a series of therapies to move on from the past.

If nothing else, simply talking to a professional will help you see things from a more objective perspective.

Examine Your Social Circle

Consider moving away from friends who compel you to live in the past. Your immediate social environment will play an essential role in helping you let go of the past. It also defines who you are and affects your experiences. An encouraging, positive and supportive social circle that doesn't make you stay in the past can change how you look at things.

I would recommend spending time with people who make you laugh or help you feel good about yourself. Stay away from folks who encourage negative habits or make you feel miserable about yourself. These are the type of people who will only stop your emotional growth or development. For instance, friends who constantly try to put you down or keep reminding you of the past may not be good news. Try making new friends in a different setting. This will get you out of your comfort zone and facilitate personal growth.

Try new hobbies with new friends. Join a hobby group on social media or a local hobby club where you can interact with people who share similar interests. New directions in life can open avenues you hadn't thought were possible earlier.

Systematic Desensitization

Systematic desensitization is a technique through which you are gradually relieving yourself of a potentially destructive situation with a series of relaxation techniques. The objective is to be at ease while exploring different stress relief methods.

Start with simple relaxation techniques such as deep breathing, exercising and meditation. Each time you find yourself exposed to a situation that stresses you as it reminds you of experience, you can practice these relaxation techniques to stay calm. The idea is to progress at your pace without rushing yourself to eliminate the pain. You should be able to engage confidently in situations that cause you to distress over some time

For instance, if you had a terrible experience while addressing an audience on the stage earlier, you may avoid all opportunities to speak on stage. An experience comes to haunt you each time you think of going on the stage. Get past this by actively opting to address an audience. Start with a small group of friends or co-workers in a meeting room or your home.

Employ relaxation techniques each time you find yourself being a bundle of nerves before speaking. Gradually, go with a bigger audience. There will come a time when you will be completely confident about addressing an audience without any fear. Keep going slowly, steadily and consistently. It may not be easy initially, but eventually, you'll gather the confidence to master the art of speaking to an audience without being nervous.

Chapter 31: The Art of Effective Communication

Besides a high level of EQ, there is one other quality that everyone should possess to help them thrive in the work environment and everyday life in general. That quality is effective communication. You could have all the most brilliant ideas, the best strategies and the best plans for success, but if you don't know how to communicate those ideas effectively, they are not going to be of much use to you. Even in everyday life, if you struggle to communicate, it can be a real challenge. It can be very stressful trying to get people to understand what you're trying to say and where you're coming from.

This is why the art of effective communication is something you need to work on improving, along with your emotional intelligence. For communication to be considered effective and successful, your message must be understood clearly. The exchange of information between two or several individuals must be clearly understood by all involved, with little or no misunderstandings happening.

Why Effective Communication Matters

How often have you thought about the way that you communicate? Give it some serious thought for a minute. Communication is a skill that many don't think twice about, but it is one of the most important skills you could have at your disposal. Effective communication matters because it helps us relate and collaborate with the people living in the world.

Effective communication is also important because:

- **It Avoids Misunderstandings** - Misunderstandings increase the chances of a conflict. This often happens when information is misconstrued or taken out of context. Why does this happen? Because there's a lack of effective communication going on. Misunderstandings can often lead to heated arguments, fights and severed relationships depending on the seriousness of the situation. If you have ever gone for weeks, months or maybe even years without speaking to someone because of a misunderstanding, you'll know exactly just how damaging this can be. Which further emphasizes why it is so important that we all work on improving our communication skills. We communicate with hundreds of people throughout our lives, every day and in the workplace. You need to be able to express your messages clearly so that it minimizes the chances that what you're going to say is going to cause problems for yourself and the people that you're speaking to.

- **It Helps You Form Powerful Relationships** - The connections that we make in life matter, especially in the career world. How well you're able to connect to other people is the foundation of all relationships. Everyone starts as strangers in the beginning, and it is through communication that those bonds are taken to another level. People start talking; you get to know each other, form connections based on mutual interest. All of this can only happen if you're able to express yourself well through effective communication. If nobody can understand what you're trying to say, it makes it harder to connect to you. For example, think of when you tried to forge a connection with someone who didn't speak the same language. Wasn't it much harder? That's a struggle you would have to deal with regularly without the power of effective communication.

- **It Boosts Your Confidence** - Successful leaders and individuals alike seem to ooze confidence on every level. When they speak, people stop and listen, transfixed by what they're saying. When they speak, people absorb what they're saying, which is how they manage to captivate large groups of audiences. That's the art of effective communication at work. When you're able to communicate effectively, your confidence level is given a tremendous boost because you do not doubt that you can express and tell people exactly what you want them to know. You find that you are no longer shy and awkward when it comes time for you to speak because you exactly know what to do and how to handle the situation. You know exactly what needs to be done. Success cannot be achieved if you're not able to convey yourself properly. If you're going to be a leader who can command large groups of people, the people must understand you effortlessly.

- **It Gives You a Leg Up In Your Career -** Our workplace is where we spend most of our day. From Monday right up to Friday, morning to evening, our lives are focused on our careers and doing our jobs. If you aspire to achieve great heights in your career, effective communication and emotional intelligence is the winning combination that you need. In the workplace, communication skills are just as vital as all the other skill sets you to need to get your job done right. Without it, it's only a matter of time before you get overtaken by those with better communication abilities. Effective communication can give you a leg up in your career because it helps you form and maintain relationships, build rapport with the people who matter. It enables you to work cohesively with people from various departments and diverse backgrounds. It helps you effectively handle both easy and difficult clients and even challenging situations. In the career world, it is all about how productive you are, and whether you're viewed as an asset to the company or the job that will put you ahead of everyone else. With a high EQ and effective communication skills at your disposal, you're already on your way to becoming a winner.

- **Helps Promote Teamwork and Innovation at the Workplace -** When you're comfortable enough to communicate your ideas at work freely, it helps to increase the level of innovation experienced. This, in turn, increases the chances of good ideas and contributions being implemented at work to improve the workflow, draw in new clients and improve the company's daily operations as a whole. When effective communication flows freely in the workplace, it is easier to build teams that are productive and cohesive, who work well together to get things done. When colleagues and different teams can come together, work well and communicate effectively with each other, staff morale is given a boost, and there's generally a more positive vibe and feel at work. Instead of dreading your job, you might even come to love it because you feel productive, and you know that you're making contributions that are only serving to improve your reputation as an employee.

Communication Barriers You Need to Overcome

For effective communication to take place, you're going to need to overcome the barriers preventing it from happening.

Communication is complex. Sometimes, despite all your efforts, misunderstandings could still occur. During the communication process, there are sometimes barriers that tend to come up that can result in poor communication. These are communication barriers.

These barriers are the reason your messages tend to become misconstrued or taken out of context. Some examples of communication barriers include:

- **Information Overload** - Not everyone processes information in the same way. If you distribute your information too fast and too soon, you could risk overwhelming the person you're speaking to because they don't have enough time to process what you're telling them.

- **Language Differences** - The world we live in today is more diverse than it has ever been. We come into contact with people from all sorts of different cultural backgrounds. While this is a wonderful thing, the different languages and accents can sometimes prove a communication barrier. Some words may be pronounced differently, or sentences become difficult to understand because of a different accent.

- **Being Distracted by External Factors -** Our mobile phones are perhaps the biggest distraction in our lives. General noise, other people are talking, phones ringing, traffic honking, messages beeping into your mobile phone, even the urge to frequently check social media is a communication barrier because it distracts you from focusing on the message that you should be receiving.

- **Making Assumptions** - We've all been guilty of jumping to conclusions even before the person we're talking to has finished what they're trying to say. This barrier occurs when you decide to reach on a course of action without fully listening to all the information first. When you make assumptions, you're mentally blocking out the rest of the message without even realizing it, tuning out and not paying attention anymore because you've already jumped ahead to what you think should be done next. You run the risk of making even more mistakes this way.

- **A Lack of Self-Confidence -** Being shy and nervous can be viewed as a communication barrier because it makes communication awkward. When you're shy, you tend to mumble, stutter or even forget a lot of what you intended to say.

- **Talking in A Hurry -** Rushing through the message puts you at risk of missing crucial information that needs to be communicated. When you speak hurriedly, you could stress out the person you're speaking to because they can't keep up with what you're trying to say.

How to Improve Your Communication Skills

To start working on becoming a more effective communicator, here is what you need to start working on and taking into account:

- **Go Right to the Point -** Being concise and specific is the best way to get your message across in the most effective manner. Communicate only the essential points, and leave out anything that is unnecessary. People have short attention spans, and this technique is the best way to ensure all the important information is conveyed the way it should be.

- **Focus on the Message -** Stay focused on the message. The more focused you are on what's important, the better you can ensure that the important information is communicated with minimal room for misunderstanding. For example, at the workplace, if you were talking about a co-worker's performance, focus on the performance aspect alone and avoid discussing unrelated matters such as their personality or the way they are dressed as an example.

- **Keep Distractions at Bay -** If you know you're about to have an important conversation, put away anything that can serve as a distraction. Put your mobile phone on silent, put it away in your pocket, find a quiet space where you can speak. Do your best to give the person your full attention and request that they do the same.

- **Be an Active Listener -** Effective communication is not just about you speaking and making yourself heard. It is about learning to be an active listener too. Communication works both ways, and for both parties to fully benefit from the conversation, you must be an equally active listener. This is where the social skills and the empathy aspect of emotional intelligence come into play because you need to be attuned to the emotions and feelings of people.

- **Speak with Clarity -** Speak clearly and confidently, and pronounce each word. Avoid meek, soft tones and especially avoid mumbling or muttering your words because nobody will be able to understand what you're saying when you do.

Conclusion

On a final note, mastering your own emotions is the surest way of advancing your social skills. Knowing that your emotions can have a huge influence on your relationships should drive you to learn how you can effectively deal with them. Individuals with high emotional intelligence know how to relate with others perfectly. These people are always careful not to let their emotions get the best of them.

Before pointing fingers at other people for your bad moods, you should understand that you are giving them control over how you feel. When you comprehend that you are the master of your own emotions, you will always be happy. Nothing will prevent you from living a happy life surrounded by people who express their love to you. Therefore, it is only through emotional intelligence that you can improve your life in all areas.

The elements of emotional intelligence tell a lot about what you need to do to boost your EQ. The first step you need to take is to be self-aware about your emotions. You cannot understand what others are feeling if you cannot comprehend your emotions. Through self-awareness, you will realize that your emotions will affect not only you but also other people. So, your EQ begins by first recognizing that it is vital for you to keep your feelings in check.

Comparably, you should work on self-managing your emotions. This demands that you should know the right manner of expressing yourself. In other words, you should know when to react and how to react depending on the situation you are faced with.

Another element of EQ is social skills. For you to consider yourself as emotionally witty, you ought to embody superior social skills. People should see you as an example of how you socialize with them. Your communication skills should define the type of person you are. More importantly, it should tell other individuals that you are an empathic person who is intrinsically motivated to succeed in life.

We all have emotions to deal with in our everyday lives. Whether at home or work, there are emotions we need to manage. This means that our style of coping with these feelings will have an impact on our lives in many ways. For instance, when one is aware of their emotional abilities, he can tune themselves to share blissful relationships with others. Happy relationships can only be shared by people who understand each other. To live a happy life with other people, you need to begin by seeking joy within you. Consequently, this means that there is a dire need for you to boost your EQ.

Increasing your emotional intelligence not only helps you create meaningful relationships with other people, but it increases your chances of succeeding in life. How is this possible? Knowing how you feel and managing your emotions will develop a positive outlook on your life. You will always have a reason to live and see the next day. The strong bonds that you create with other people will motivate you to value experiences over material things. Your innate motivation will drive you to perceive life in ways that other people might not understand. To you, succeeding will not be an option but a necessity in your life.

Mastering your emotions will indeed bring many benefits to your life. Besides fostering meaningful relationships in your life, you will always gain from the desirable values you will be generating.